Praise for
Gardening Eden

"Firmly one of the most socially relevant topics today, environmentalism elicits a variety of intense reactions. Michael Abbaté's book lifts creation care above the typical debate and gets back to its appropriate starting point—on our knees, in awe of the Creator. His passion for God and affection for creation is evident throughout, while weaving together science, Scripture, and personal experiences, with probing and comfort-squashing questions. As he advocates for worship, he also provides numerous practical, and even easy, tips for caring for creation that has me thinking far beyond energy efficient light bulbs and my stellar compost pile."

—TIM OSBORN, lead pastor, Mosaic Church, Portland, OR, www.mosaicportland.org

"This is a book Christians should read! Though our primary task is to carry out the Great Commission while on this earth, we must not neglect the place God created for us to live."

—DR. GENE A. GETZ, president, Center for Church Renewal; host, Renewal Radio, Dallas, TX

"Evangelicals will be well informed and morally challenged to tend the garden without being throttled. And, progressives will be thrilled to hear the Christian call to care for the earth. Where was this two decades prior? I give my evangelical and progressive, two green thumbs up!"

—REV. LEROY HEDMAN, Georgetown Gospel Chapel, Seattle, WA

"Michael Abbaté's book *Gardening Eden* offers a sound, compelling. and practical approach to 'Creation Care.' As people seeking to become better 'gardeners' ourselves, we appreciated Michael's style and approach and wholeheartedly recommend this book!"

—MIKE AND DANAE YANKOSKI, authors
of *Under the Overpass*

How Creation Care
Will Change
Your Faith, Your Life,
and Our World

Gardening Eden

Michael
Abbaté

WATERBROOK
PRESS

GARDENING EDEN
PUBLISHED BY WATERBROOK PRESS
12265 Oracle Boulevard, Suite 200
Colorado Springs, Colorado 80921

All Scripture quotations, unless otherwise indicated, are taken from the Holy Bible, New International Version®. NIV®. Copyright © 1973, 1978, 1984 by International Bible Society. Used by permission of Zondervan Publishing House. All rights reserved. Scripture quotations marked (NASB) are taken from the New American Standard Bible®. © Copyright The Lockman Foundation 1960, 1962, 1963, 1968, 1971, 1972, 1973, 1975, 1977, 1995. Used by permission. (www.Lockman.org). Scripture quotations marked (NKJV) are taken from the New King James Version®. Copyright © 1982 by Thomas Nelson Inc. Used by permission. All rights reserved. Scripture quotations marked (NLT) are taken from the Holy Bible, New Living Translation, copyright © 1996. Used by permission of Tyndale House Publishers Inc., Wheaton, Illinois 60189. All rights reserved.

Italics in Scripture quotations reflect the author's added emphasis.

ISBN 978-0-30744-499-8

ISBN 978-0-30744-600-8 (electronic)

Opening poem in Chapter 1 copyright © 2004 by Ted Kooser, "On the Road" from *Delights & Shadows*. Reprinted with permission of Copper Canyon Press, www.coppercanyonpress.org.

Opening quote in Chapter 2 copyright © 2006 by Wendell Berry from *The Unforeseen Wilderness*. Reprinted with permission of Counterpoint.

Published in the United States by WaterBrook Multnomah, an imprint of The Doubleday Publishing Group, a division of Random House Inc., New York.

WATERBROOK and its deer colophon are registered trademarks of Random House Inc.

Library of Congress Cataloging-in-Publication Data
Abbaté, Michael.
    Gardening Eden : how creation care will change your life, your faith, and our world / Michael Abbate.—1st ed.
        p. cm.
        ISBN 978-0-30744-499-8—ISBN 978-0-30744-600-8 1. Human ecology—Religious aspects—Christianity. 2. Ecotheology. I. Title.
        BT695.5.A23 2009
        261.8'8—dc22

                                        2008045790

Printed in the United States of America
2009—First Edition

10 9 8 7 6 5 4 3 2 1

SPECIAL SALES
Most WaterBrook Multnomah books are available in special quantity discounts when purchased in bulk by corporations, organizations, and special-interest groups. Custom imprinting or excerpting can also be done to fit special needs. For information, please e-mail SpecialMarkets@WaterBrookMultnomah.com or call 1-800-603-7051.

For Brooke's and Maryn's grandchildren:
May you find creation healthier than at the beginning
of the twenty-first century and love the Creator even more
than your great-grandfather.

Contents

Contents

Foreword

by Randy Alcorn

A few weeks ago, I spoke at a conference of several thousand evangelical college students. Most were from Bible-believing churches like my own.

My message concerned the promise of a New Earth and the biblical principle of continuity. From Scripture, I pointed out that just as our old bodies will be destroyed, then made new in the resurrection, so the old earth will be destroyed, and then made into a New Earth. Next I cited Genesis 1 concerning God's original job description for human beings living on this planet. I'll break right into the message here, quoting directly from the audio transcript, so you know exactly what I said (it's important to the story):

> ...and God saw that it was good. And then God said, "Let us make man in our image, in our likeness, and let them rule over the fish of the sea and the birds of the air, over the livestock, over all the earth."
>
> This was God's purpose: that we rule the earth as His image-bearers to His glory; that we would care for the animals, and do the other things that we do in the development of culture.
>
> So God created man in His own image, and God said to them, "Be fruitful and increase in number (not just the two of you; it's going to be a world full of people); fill the earth and subdue it."

This word "subdue" is not a negative word. It doesn't mean we shouldn't be concerned for the environment. And by the way, of all people, as stewards, don't you think we ought to have reasonable concern for our environment and try to take care of it?

I hadn't planned to ask that question, but I did. Suddenly somebody applauded. Now, at conferences, if you ask a question to a crowd and there's widespread agreement, often enthusiastic applause erupts as a way of saying "yes." If there's moderate agreement, there's moderate applause. But even if relatively few agree, there's an unspoken etiquette whereby some give a token applause, if nothing else to rescue the lone clapper! But that day something remarkable happened. Nobody else clapped! The solitary clapper suddenly stopped, as if to say, "Oops… never mind." (Ever had that feeling when you realize, in a crowd of people, you're the *only* one laughing?)

As I continued speaking, I joked about the awkward moment, saying, "Wow! Someone started to applaud!" I was alluding to the fact that it was surprising that anyone would applaud a pro-environment statement at a conservative evangelical gathering. (By the way, I am thoroughly evangelical and in some political issues conservative.)

Now, trust me, it didn't hurt my feelings that no one else applauded. Those attending this conference were very warm and responsive to my messages. No problem there.

But here's my point: these people were serious Christians attending a Christ-exalting, Bible-believing, and Bible-teaching conference. Yet even the peer pressure exerted by that one individual clapping failed to elicit applause from so much as one other person. *Why?*

I think the answer is that the great majority of those present were not only theologically conservative, but socially and politically conservative. And concern for the environment is generally regarded as part of the *liberal* agenda. What *sounds* socially liberal *sounds* theologically liberal. And, understandably, biblical conservatives don't want to sound liberal.

I'm politically conservative on issues such as abortion, in which lives are at stake. But I am also concerned about the welfare of the environment God has entrusted to our care (in which, by the way, human lives are also at stake). I see absolutely no contradiction between the two positions. In fact, they are a perfect fit.

I believe that even if concern for the environment makes us "sound liberal" to some, we should be willing to express it because God says we are the caretakers of His creation. That is our biblical job description, our divine calling from the beginning. It shouldn't matter whether caring for the poor or caring for the environment is considered conservative or liberal. Who cares? We should seek to be biblical and Christ-centered, loving God and our neighbor, and not worrying about labels and who else does or doesn't agree with us on a given issue.

I trust there were many young people in that audience concerned about caring for the environment. Many of them might have joined the applause had someone made the comment on their college campus. But I believe their conservative evangelical conditioning did not allow them freedom to affirm that conviction. Even though I made my comment about the environment based on Scripture, it did not seem safe or appropriate to join the applause. Had I spoken in defense of the unborn, which I have on many occasions, if one person had applauded that day, I guarantee others would have followed (unlike the deafening silence you'd hear on most secular college campuses).

Let me just say it: care for the environment is not something that can be comfortably applauded in many Bible-believing church contexts. It is not a popular subject.

I believe this needs to change. We need to be part of cultivating a new biblical peer pressure that is pro-creation. Mike Abbaté's fine book *Gardening Eden* can be part of that change.

For too long, evangelical Christians have neglected our God-given calling to care for the planet entrusted to us. One reason may be that our eschatology indicates the earth is headed for ruin anyway, so there's no point in trying to rearrange the furniture on the *Titanic*. Well, I too believe that the present earth will come to an end, as graphically described in 2 Peter 3. But God made this earth, and He promises us a New Earth.

It makes no sense to say that because the earth will be destroyed, therefore we shouldn't take good care of it! Do we argue that because our bodies will be destroyed we shouldn't take good care of them? What would you say to your teenager if you warned him not to smoke, and he replied, "But it doesn't matter, because the Bible says we're going to die anyway"?

God entrusts us with the earth as He entrusts us with our bodies, and He intends for us to take care of both. If you are conservative, then doesn't it make sense to try to conserve your own health, your family's health, and the health of the world we inhabit? (That "conservation" became a *liberal* term instead of a *conservative* one is counterintuitive.)

Perhaps because many environmental activists scorn the Bible and Christian beliefs, we have ignored our stewardship job description, as if it were somehow incompatible with the gospel. But it was God, not an environmental extremist, who delegated to us the responsibility of creation care. It was *God,* not an animal rights activist, who entrusted animals to us. Just as John 3:16 is inspired by God, so is Proverbs 12:10: "A righteous man cares for the needs of his animal."

I have pointed out to people the inconsistency of their outrage that baby seals are being cruelly clubbed to death, while they defend the fact that baby human beings are being cruelly ripped apart in their mothers' wombs. We *should* oppose cruelty to baby animals, *and* we should oppose even more cruelty to baby humans.

I stand with my friends, believers and unbelievers, who are concerned for the poor and the environment, even though we sometimes disagree on the best policies related to helping both. God's Word makes clear His passion for the poor and His appointment of us as the caretakers of the earth. If I am a Bible-believing Christian, then these matters simply *must* concern me.

True, we cannot return this world to Eden. Yes, we should be looking forward to the New Earth, which God alone can make. (We humans have proven miserable failures when it comes to utopia-building.) Absolutely, human beings are more important than snail darters and spotted owls.

But we should still be caring for this earth under the curse. While it groans awaiting redemption, as Romans 8 says, we need to be all the more careful to steward it with wisdom. We do this not because we owe our existence to Mother Earth, but because we owe our lives and eternal destinies to our Father God, and we owe it to Him to care for His earth.

You do not have to like or agree with Ralph Nader or Al Gore in order to care about God's creation. You can disagree, as scientists do, on the subject of the causes and effects of global warming. But Christians have no business dismissing everyone who cares about this planet as "environmental wackos" or "eco-Nazis," cranks and chicken littles. Yes, of course there are extremists. (Hey, I live in Oregon. I know those extremists, but I still want Oregon to remain clean and beautiful!) Remember, there are "Christian wackos" too, but most of us do not appreciate being dismissed by that label. Don't throw out the baby of responsible earth-care with the bathwater of anti-enterprise gloom.

In *Gardening Eden,* my friend Mike Abbaté has done a wonderful job drawing attention to our calling to care for the earth. His book is well researched and readable, engaging and valuable. There is a directness, focus, and passion to *Gardening Eden,* coupled with a rational and thoughtful consideration of others.

This book in your hands is not written by someone on the radical fringe, out of touch with the modern world. From the day Mike first met with me to share his vision for this book, I could see that he is smart and savvy, wise and articulate. Mike is a skilled professional, a landscape architect and a city planner, an accomplished expert in his field. In fact, he's now planning director of Gresham, Oregon, the city I live in and where I was raised. He is also a Bible believer and a committed follower of Jesus. Good for him that he takes so seriously the sacred task of stewarding God's earth. I am delighted to stand with him.

As you read Mike's book, keep in mind God's Word: "The earth is the LORD's, and everything in it, the world, and all who live in it" (Psalm 24:1). This is not our place to trash. It's God's place to treasure. To care for the world is to care for its people. To take care of people is to fulfill the second greatest commandment, to love our neighbors as ourselves. In doing so we also obey the greatest commandment, to love God with all our hearts.

"The LORD rejoices in all he has made!" (Psalm 104:31, NLT). If He rejoices in it, so should we. When you rejoice in something, you go out of your way to preserve it.

Proverbs 21:20 says, "In the house of the wise are stores of choice food and oil, but a foolish man devours all he has." Foolish people consume; wise people preserve, understanding that even if we die tomorrow, we should leave something behind for our children and our children's children, and the generations that may follow. The earth is not disposable. Nor are its resources inexhaustible.

Creation care makes good sense even if it were not explicitly stated in our job description. But read Genesis 1 and 2, and you will see that it clearly is.

If I told you I loved my children but allowed open gas lines in the house, removed the smoke detectors, and let broken windows go unfixed, you would have reason to question my parenting. Why? Because if a parent loves his children, he'll do his best to provide them a safe home.

God never revoked His plan to entrust the earth's care to us. Romans 8 makes clear that the whole creation fell on our coattails, and, in our resurrection, will rise on our coattails—all the more reason that we should care for it.

Now, my discretionary stewardship decisions may look quite different from yours. You don't have to do it my way; I don't have to do it yours. Legalism in creation care is as stifling and ineffective as all other legalism. But together as Christ-centered, Bible-believing, people-loving Christians we should agree to be creation-loving. We shouldn't have to follow secular culture in reasonable creation care; we should lead the way. And when people ask why we care about the planet, we should be ready to tell them we love this world because we love its Creator and Redeemer.

I love the fact that Mike Abbaté doesn't leave us on the theoretical level but offers specific suggestions for creation care, right down to alternatives in growing and buying food. Mike is not using this book to make extreme claims or pick a fight or take political sides. This is not a political book that stereotypes or berates people or assumes the worst of them. If you find some things in the book you disagree with, fine. You don't have to wear a Tree Hugger T-shirt. (I don't.) We can still disagree about which government policies will and will not help care for the environment, as long as we are truly committed to caring for the environment.

Gardening Eden contains good theology, worldview, science, and practical application. This book is fair and balanced, demonstrating an unapologetic love for God's creation, something conservatives and liberals alike should share. It is a welcome and much-needed resource, whose time has come. I pray it will open the minds and hearts of many to the privileges and responsibilities of stewarding God's world.

Now, let me finish my story. After speaking at the evangelical youth conference that day, I stayed and spoke with many students who were wonderfully responsive. Afterward, as my wife, Nanci, and I headed to lunch, I smiled and said to her, "Wasn't that something when that poor person applauded and nobody else joined in?"

Nanci, eyes big, replied, "That poor person who applauded was *me*!"

Well, Nanci, I know you will applaud Mike Abbaté's book. And I hope you, the reader, will join in applauding the notion that we should be thoughtful caretakers of God's creation. Not *in spite of* the fact that we believe the Bible and trust Jesus, but precisely *because* we do.

Part I

The Garden State

"They Do Not Care"

ON THE ROAD

By the toe of my boot,

a pebble of quartz,

one drop of the earth's milk,

dirty and cold.

I held it to the light

and could almost see through it

into the grand explanation.

Put it back, something told me,

put it back and keep walking.

—TED KOOSER, U.S. Poet Laureate,
Delights & Shadows

I t's remarkable the things people will tell you when they consider you a stranger. I suppose we all bring our preconceptions when we meet someone, assuming they think just like we do.

Recently I was invited to speak at a university in the Midwest on the topic of designing sustainable campuses and communities. The people who invited me were curious about some of the projects our firm had been involved with on the West Coast. They hoped to learn lessons they could apply locally.

It was February, and after arriving in the frigid subarctic temperature, I set about getting my bearings and willing my blood to thicken. In the three days leading up to my talk, a guide toured me around the university, the city, and the surrounding rural area. She was a wonderfully energetic and passionate biology professor, and she hoped my talk could be a catalyst for change in the community. Her commitment to protecting the earth was deep, and she longed for others to catch a vision of ways the community could be transformed into one that cared about "proper ecological stewardship."

As we visited snow-covered parks and natural areas, the frozen winter air invading my lungs, I became aware of the shortcomings of my wardrobe. Hailing from the Pacific Northwest, I had Gore-Tex, but not enough woolen padding for the bright, crystalline world in which I found myself. We warmed up in local restaurants, where I was honored to meet many of her academic friends who shared her passion for improving their community and flattered me with their excited attention.

I soon found that my professor friend's passions for ecology transcended the physical world and extended to the spiritual as well. She felt that the religion of Christianity—indeed, Christians themselves—were responsible for the vast majority of environmental degradation worldwide. She ridiculed believers, the four Christian colleges in her city, and the churches and denominational headquarters located there. "They deny global warming," she said. "They do not care about species going extinct. They're more concerned with their own comfort than they are with clean water and air for future generations." These were her decided conclusions.

On the third morning, she exclaimed, "I'm a recovering Southern Baptist." I looked at her, waiting for the explanation or the punch line. "I was a dyed-in-the-wool creationist until my fourth year of college, when I finally saw the evolutionary light." Evolutionary light. This was her phrase. And then she launched into another attack on the hypocrites who claim to love one another but refuse to support efforts to protect the environment.

The complaints were not new to me, and they certainly were not without foundation. In fact, the very same convictions have been pivotal in prodding me along on my own ecological-spiritual journey.

Each of her comments jabbed my psyche. I was weary of the diatribes and wanted to say, "The choice between faith and the environment is a false dichotomy. You don't have to choose secularism to care about creation." But I held my tongue. I barely knew her, and I reminded myself that one person's strong opinions aren't generally improved by another's.

As we rode in her Subaru through downtown neighborhoods, past buildings and parks, it became clear that she assumed I shared her deep convictions about the irreconcilable difference between ecological concerns and Christian faith. To her, my silence was assent.

The day of my presentation arrived and, with it, the university community awaiting my thoughts. The auditorium began to fill with students thirty minutes early, but I was surprised by the number of community leaders, city staff, and local professionals who gathered as well. The room was soon filled to capacity, with people standing in the rear and along the sides.

I began with self-evident truths. There are many reasons why it makes sense to plan, design, and build in ways that are compatible with the natural systems of the planet. All of these reasons—protecting the earth for our descendants, alleviating suffering, ensuring species continuance, helping the economy—are appropriate reasons to respond to living in harmony with our environment.

However, I said, these same concerns can arise from two quite distinct worldviews.

Secular humanists believe that we must not do anything to disrupt the natural evolutionary process already taking place all around us. We must ensure that we do not harm the earth's ability to support all living things in the future. E.O. Wilson, the Pulitzer Prize–winning biologist, is a compelling advocate of this worldview:

> Earth provides a self-regulating bubble that sustains us indefinitely without any thought or contrivance on our own. This protective shield is the biosphere.... Upon its delicate health we depend for every moment of our lives.[1]

---

1. E. O. Wilson, *The Creation: An Appeal to Save Life on Earth* (New York: W. W. Norton, 2006), 27.

In fact, Wilson recognizes the important link between faith and conservation, though he isn't a Christian. *"We will not reach our full potential without understanding the origin and hence meaning of the aesthetic and religious qualities that make us ineffably human."*

The second worldview, I explained, comes from the first book of the Bible. Up flashed these words on the screen: "The LORD God took the man and put him in the Garden of Eden to work it and take care of it" (Genesis 2:15).

I mentioned that this initial directive has not been a topic of much emphasis in Christian circles, nor in any of the other major world religions, for that matter. For much of the last century, religious institutions have missed—or ignored—our responsibility as stewards of the creation and to the Creator. However, people of faith have long relished the grimy pleasures of gardening. The process of nurturing life brings contentment and a sense of wholeness in the accomplishment. We instinctively understand that we were designed to be gentle gardeners. We just haven't realized that the entire planet is our garden.

I went on to share some of my ideas for conservation and sustainability, and following my talk, a number of people came forward to tell me that they had never heard faith mentioned as a reason for environmental stewardship. I explained that, in fact, it was the original reason, and the Christians among them were appreciative. As people filed out, I looked around for my passionate friend. She was nowhere in sight. I hoped she wasn't deeply offended. She was to be my ride back to the airport.

• • •

Everywhere we go, we see and hear of impending ecological catastrophe. Global climate change, holes in the ozone layer, extinction of species, hurricanes, deforestation, and starvation caused by drought and pollution all compete for our attention. What do we make of this situation? Are our lives impacting, even causing these global issues? Surely we are not responsible for the dodo birds and the woolly mammoths, are we?

Sometimes it's a matter of our survival to dismiss these distressing headlines. We're just trying to get through another day. Still, we know there's more to life than survival.

When the shift came for me, I was in the process of getting through my hitch in the navy. I had my whole life ahead of me. My concerns were with figuring out who to live life with, what I was going to do for a living, what type of education I would need, and where I would live. My definition of "the future" encompassed just under five years.

But an amazing thing happened to me on my way to the future.

My wife and I created another human being. Brooke, the first of our two daughters, arrived on the scene announcing that a change in our outlook was in store. In an instant, time was redefined. The future suddenly extended beyond me and my immediate needs. Three years later, her sister, Maryn, joined the refrain, and these two new lives initiated a chorus demanding profound change in me. Suddenly, "the future" stretched far beyond five years. In fact, I was able to see ahead a generation, to the time when my daughters were my age. I noticed that along with my new expansive power, a new realization of weakness grabbed at my heel. *What sort of world am I leaving for their inheritance?*

My worries about one-dollar gas prices vaporized and were replaced by images of a smog-choked, barren landscape where most elements of life—air, water, land—were irrevocably damaged. The future felt suddenly close. It mattered. Where the world seemed headed was not a place I wanted my girls to be. When you wrap your arms around an infant, maybe you can see this way too. What lies ahead for him or her?

As I sit here today, nearly half a century has migrated from the future into the past for me. And once again, I notice that the passing of time only expands our vision of the future. Grandchildren are coming, and terrifyingly, great-grandchildren are imaginable. Now, instead of seeing only twenty years ahead, I am wondering about half a century. This is quite a disconcerting paradox; the older I get, the further into the future I can see.

And the future takes on new meaning. I find myself less concerned about my life today and more anxious about tomorrow for those I love. Today's headlines become more ominous, not because I will be affected, but because they will be. A new reality has gripped me and, perhaps, you as well: our daily stewardship of this planet is our down payment for our children's children's children. Anyone with more potent time-traveling powers than I had at twenty might draw the same conclusions.

• • •

After my talk, I grabbed my luggage and waited in the lobby. In a few minutes, the biology professor pulled up and jumped out to help me load the car for our ride to the airport.

"That was a wonderful talk," she stated flatly as we drove along. Realizing the wall she'd been building between us for the past few days, she began to knock it down, brick by brick. She shared more about her background and the thoughts she'd been having about the link between faith and stewardship, and then she looked at me with new eyes. "You know, our university chaplain has asked me to come and talk about protecting the environment." She nodded and added, a bit more enthusiastically, "I really enjoyed your perspective on bringing together the spiritual and the physical."

"Thank you. That's wonderful," I said, meaning it.

Another benefit of age: the older I get, the more I appreciate life's surprises. It occurred to me we had a lot more in common than either of us realized. Later, as I considered our final conversation more, I realized she had helped me discover a bridge across the divide between faith and environmentalism. And for that I was more than grateful.

11

2

Building the Bridge

THE ONE-INCH JOURNEY

And the world cannot be discovered by a journey
of miles, no matter how long, but only by a spiritual
journey, a journey of one inch, very arduous and
humbling and joyful, by which we arrive at the
ground at our feet, and learn to be at home.

—WENDELL BERRY,
The Unforeseen Wilderness

Growing up in the prototypical suburbs of Southern California, I spent my younger years roaming the streets and parks of Alhambra, San Gabriel, Temple City, and Arcadia. On my bike, I discovered the incredible diversity of the San Gabriel Valley. I used to love sneaking into the Los Angeles County Arboretum, that 127-acre oasis in the middle of my paved, suburban world. There I could lose myself in the bamboo forest, chase peacocks, or explore the prehistoric jungle garden where scenes from *Fantasy Island, Tarzan,* and so many other Hollywood television series were filmed. And when I was caught hitching a ride on the back of the visitor tram, I was always escorted to the front gate by the disapproving staff.

But the best fun was visiting my grandparents' house in San Gabriel. I spent a lot of time at Mimi and Pop's. The barbecues on the back patio were always a favorite. But my grandparents' modest postwar ranch house wasn't the real attraction for me. My grandfather called it "the back forty"—the slope below the patio that seemed to stretch downhill for at least a quarter mile. It was actually only a couple hundred feet, but covered with huge eucalyptus trees and a tangle of understory shrubs, it was a natural paradise to a young boy, a place of discovery and adventure. Raccoons, skunks, and a semi-tame blue jay

I named Pete made this my very own garden of Eden. I found rotting logs to build forts with and spent hours digging, building, and observing the natural world around me.

Years later I learned that it wasn't really all that "natural." At the base of the hill was a chain-link fence preventing me from falling into the river below. And the river was actually the concrete Alhambra wash flood-control channel. Twenty feet deep and thirty feet across, it was off-limits to me, though I dreamed of the things I heard of other kids doing—like riding their bikes down the wide channel for miles. I recall adults recounting stories of kids killed by surprise flood waters that rushed down the wash, which only made it sound all the more exciting.

But for me, experiencing nature in the back forty was like what other kids experienced playing in the "crick" or exploring the swamp or hiking in the woods or riding motorcycles in the desert. This was my education in the beauty and harsh realities of nature. Watch your step, or you'll be up to your knees in muck. Be quiet, or you'll scare off that beautiful bird. Be patient. Be watchful. Be ready.

Giant, dewy spider webs like crystal necklaces, a trout rising to snatch a caddisfly off the surface, a doe feeding in the meadow beyond (your heart pounding loud enough to scare her away). For kids fortunate enough to experience these moments, it's natural to fall in love with nature. Even wilderness emergencies educate and excite young minds as nature draws us with a force we can't deny.

Four decades later, I realize I was always strongly and consistently fascinated by the world around me. The more times I watched *Mutual of Omaha's Wild Kingdom,* the more I felt drawn to experience nature for myself. But in adolescence, I became one more teenager adrift, with little motivation and a taste for trouble.

Fortunately, my path made a slight detour to the mountains. It's only fitting that I first felt drawn to God at a summer high school camp in the crisp, thin air of the Sierra Nevada. For the first time in my life, I heard that I didn't have to struggle alone with the problems in my life. The Creator of the universe was not punishing me. On the contrary, He loved me enough to take on my problems. He actually had a purpose and plan for me, and He wanted me to be fully alive and fulfilled. My soul soaked up this new truth like a desert soaks up a summer rain. He grabbed my attention, convinced me of His reality, and told me that I was worthy of His eternal love. Seeds of hope began to germinate. My life was about to take a new direction and become a life filled with faith. It's a similar story for millions—a supernatural intervention at a critical time.

There I turned down a different path. I became more interested in eternity. But one thing did not change—my appreciation of nature. If anything, with my new understanding of the Creator, it grew.

Yet for much of my adult life, I've lived in two worlds. My vocational world is landscape architecture and city planning where design progresses with an intentionally physical emphasis and humanistic perspective. Optimistic, idealistic, with high expectations for the human capacity to improve the world, the people I work with are concerned with the environmental condition. These are the great people I am surrounded by every day, and I've been fortunate to be inspired by them in my pursuits.

My other foot lands solidly in the faith camp, the community of evangelical Christians. Here I also find people who inspire me but in a different way, a spiritual way. I've met hundreds of people who gladly make incredible sacrifices for others, people living lives of genuine faith full of mercy and love. And as in my professional circle, they're involved in many causes and organizations. Their focus tends to be on issues that improve the physical and spiritual condition of the poorest of the poor, and good pours out of them in their genuine gratitude to God for His blessings. Their service expresses their worship and thanks to God.

However, as I became more and more established in Christian culture, I began to notice an interesting dichotomy: though most of my Christian friends enjoyed the outdoors, very few were concerned about the environmental headlines of the day. I rarely found anyone who believed that the condition of the planet itself was important to God.

We all inhabit the same planet. I wonder if the issue of creation care might bring these two worldviews together to till common ground.

Until now the humanists and idealists have viewed those interested in faith and spiritual matters as largely foreign, and vice versa. But is the divide a real one? Or is it just illusion? Must environmentalists automatically dismiss God? Do people of faith have to forfeit protecting the environment to serve God?

A nationwide 2005 Harris Poll found that 74 percent of U.S. adults agreed that "protecting the environment is so important that requirements and standards cannot be too high, and continuing environmental improvements must be made regardless of cost." In addition, 70 percent of respondents considered themselves either sympathetic to environmental concerns or active environmentalists.[1]

But what about issues of faith? The 2008 U.S. Religious Landscape Survey indicated that 83 percent of Americans affiliate themselves with a religious tradition or group. The highest proportion, 78 percent, consider themselves Christian, with the remainder identifying them-

---

1. *The Harris Poll #77*, October 13, 2005, www.harrisinteractive.com/harris_poll/index .asp?PID=607.

selves as Jewish, Muslim, Buddhist, or of other faith traditions. Only about 17 percent of Americans identify themselves as secular or non-religious.[2]

With about three out of four Americans believing that environmental protection is an important issue, and a similar percentage considering themselves people of faith, it appears that a majority of Americans, somewhere between 50 percent and 75 percent, consider themselves interested in the environment *and* believe in God. The 2008 Pew Forum study points out that, though they're often assumed to be strongly opposed to environmental protection, a solid majority of evangelical Christians supported the statement that "tougher environmental laws are worth the cost." And yet, people of faith are rarely recognized for leading the way in promoting environmental moderation, protection, or restoration. Many nonbelieving friends and colleagues have rightly pointed this out to me as they ask, "Why aren't Christians more involved in environmental issues?"

I consider it inarguable that creation itself must play a role in the vast preponderance of people who consider themselves people of faith. Stand on the precipice of the Grand Canyon, amongst the wildflowers of an alpine meadow, or a on beach at sunset, and you think, "This can be no accident." As the apostle Paul said:

> For since the creation of the world God's invisible qualities—his eternal power and divine nature—have been clearly seen, being understood from what has been made, so that men are without excuse. (Romans 1:20)

---

2. "U.S. Religious Landscape Survey," The Pew Forum on Religion & Public Life (February 2008), http://religions.pewforum.org/pdf/report-religious-landscape-study-full.pdf.

And yet instead, the most visible leaders in the conservation movement seem to approach the issue from a scientific and secular perspective. Why is this so? The people most committed to protecting the environment are not overtly driven by a personal belief in what C.S. Lewis describes as the "something which is directing the universe." In fact, as Bill Cooke stated in *Free Inquiry,* the magazine of the Council for Secular Humanism: "The basic ethical consequence of scientific naturalism [another term for secular humanism] is that we don't matter to the universe."[3]

It's a great irony—two great ironies, in fact. Secular humanism doesn't offer a higher rationale for its convictions, and people of faith recognize no moral imperative to protect the planet. It appears something is rather wrong here.

Dispassionate Ecology Versus Disinterested Christianity

Today's evolutionary ecologists fervently advocate that we should protect the wide range of species on the planet. However, when explaining *why* we should do this, they often cite the humanistic principle that the environment sustains the human race. A quote from E.O. Wilson illustrates this stance:

> It follows that human self-interest is best served by not overtly harming the other life forms on Earth that still survive. Environmental damage can be defined as any change that alters

---

3. Bill Cooke, "Religion's Anthropocentric Conceit: Atheism's cosmic modesty is more moral," *Free Inquiry* 24, no. 1 (December 2003/January 2004).

our surroundings in a direction contrary to humanity's inborn physical and emotional needs.[4]

Should we justify protecting the planet simply because it's good for humans? From this worldview, what is "good"? Of what moral consequence is the survival of humankind? Charles Darwin was not concerned about the extinction of any particular species; in fact, he stated that extinction was a normal part of evolutionary processes. Species face elimination because of their inability to adapt to change to geologic, climatic, or ecologic forces. Should the human race be considered differently? If so, on what grounds?

Exploiting the planet's resources to the point of exhaustion and sealing our doom as a species cannot be labeled a "bad" thing from the secular perspective. In fact, it might even be considered a good thing since it would affirm natural selection at work and allow the earth to continue flourishing unimpeded. Evolution is a system of blind forces at work with no value judgments of "good" or "bad." If humans are supplanted by ants, coyotes, or some yet-to-evolve new creature, as Cooke said, "we do not matter to the universe."

In the end, I find this view of evolutionary ecology offering very little in the way of compelling answers to why we should protect the environment.

On the other side, the Christian worldview holds that humans have special, unparalleled significance in the universe. From this perspective, it matters if humans disappear from the earth and it would be a great tragedy for us to destroy ourselves by destroying our world. It would be morally "bad" to eliminate the earth's support of human life.

4. E. O. Wilson, *The Creation* (New York: W. W. Norton, 2006), 27.

To those of us who accept this view, we also acknowledge that the source of this unique status is an omnipotent Creator. We are not just one of many species, yet neither are we able to anoint ourselves with this special status. We can no more decree ourselves superior than a rock could vote itself president. This idea has led us to find meaning and purpose beyond ourselves. Yet we're not sure what to make of the physical world. Is it simply ours to use and enjoy however we choose? Or are there responsibilities involved? Do we share a duty to care for the creation?

Here's that irony again. People of faith claim to know the Artist but lack any compunction for protecting the artwork. Why have God followers not been defending this masterpiece from degradation?

We may feel nagging twinges of guilt as we look at the world around us and see the impacts of urban sprawl, industrial expansion, consumerism, and man-made disasters. We can't help worrying about tales of famine and hunger or disease from contaminated water and toxic air. But people of faith are uncertain how, or even *if,* they should respond.

Still, divergent views are not limited to these two polar groups. This dialogue is surfacing within the community of faith as well. Believers don't necessarily agree on the environmental issues of the day, such as global warming, but differing positions must be subject to informed conclusions. We must listen to others, consider their rationales, study God's Word, pray for insight, and be open to learning that may prompt us to change our opinions. Of course, skepticism is warranted when it comes to claims of impending environmental calamities. As my spiritually minded brother-in-law has told me, "It comes down to who you're willing to believe." But it seems too many Christians are using political excuses to dismiss the reasoned arguments of professionals.

Some discount Al Gore and others who warn of global warming and an impending water-supply catastrophe. It's no secret that the environmental movement is dominated by folks who don't share the Judeo-Christian worldview. On the other side of the spectrum, environmentalists are skeptical of oil-company executives who deny the links between burning carbon-based fuels, air pollution, and global warming. Record oil-company profits lead many corporations to downplay the impacts of their industry on the environment, though this has begun to shift. In September 2006, John Hofmeister, president of Shell Oil Company, said that as far as his company was concerned, the debate over the science of global climate change is settled and the evidence is incontrovertible. "It's a waste of time to debate it," he said. "We need to change the hearts, minds, values, and behavior of Americans toward a culture of conservation."[5]

Yet Mr. Hofmeister's is a lonely voice in a big industry whose reluctance to admit the environmental impacts of its practices on the environment has bred widespread distrust.

Virtually all scientists agree that climate change is happening. But the cause of this change is disputed by scientists. Al Gore's documentary *An Inconvenient Truth* outlined reasons why many believe that human activity is responsible for the increase in greenhouse gases and the resulting global warming. Yet other popular messages, including Martin Durkin's *The Great Global Warming Swindle,* contend that increased greenhouse gases are an effect rather than the cause. Whom should we believe? For many people, confusion leads to inaction. Yet it's not necessary to have complete agreement with any one point of view to be good stewards of our planet. We don't have to accept a political point of view or oppose another to be advocates for the environment.

---

5. "Oil executive rips U.S. on warming strategy," Associated Press, September 8, 2006.

The politicization of the environmental debate does not solve anyone's problem.

Both sides can debate the cause and severity of the earth's environmental problems and forecasts of the future. But in the face of competing data, are we in danger of losing sight of the real goal? Groups such as the Evangelical Environmental Network (www.creationcare.org) and the Cornwall Alliance for the Stewardship of Creation (www.corn wallalliance.org) come to different conclusions about the state of the environment and are supported by varied church leaders and academics. Yet in spite of these disagreements, are we missing a huge opportunity to replace confusion and inaction with, if not complete agreement, at least action?

It's vital that we look and think beyond the constraints of political platforms. Spiritually minded people are invited to look to their faith, not political parties or leaders, to guide their lifestyle choices. As Reverend Richard Cizik told Bill Moyers in the 2006 documentary "Is God Green?": "I happen to think that to be biblically consistent means you have to, at times, be politically inconsistent."[6]

Tilling Our Common Ground

We may (or may not) be at a crossroads in human history. Young people today are asking tough questions of scientists and theologians alike: "Is there more to the universe than matter and energy?" "Why aren't we doing more to respect the Creator in the way we treat creation?"

Friends, I believe it's time we considered our environmental discussion and efforts as a *bridge.* Today's environmental headlines, green

---

6. Tom Casciato and Bill Moyers, *Moyers on America* series, "Is God Green?" a production of Public Affairs Television Inc. and a national presentation of Thirteen/WNET New York, 2006.

initiatives, and poll results are testimony to the fact that this issue of concern to the vast majority of people, both secular and faithful, is not going away. Nor should it. All our respective communities have been presented with a unique opportunity to have an impact on something that nearly everyone cares about, with a faith that offers hope for the future.

We need to discover what our faith has to say about the issue of environmental stewardship. As God followers, we're convinced that our faith is relevant to the issues of the day, but we remain unclear about God's perspective on the environment. Does the Bible discuss global warming, water pollution, and species extinction? Or are we on our own to surmise what God might think?

25

• • •

But let's start at the beginning. Instead of asking, "Is global warming our fault?" let's focus on some more general and personally relevant questions:

- Do I have a responsibility to protect the planet?
- Are some of my current actions having a detrimental effect on the environment?
- Should I make changes to better steward the resources we have been given?

I firmly believe that if we can sufficiently answer these questions, we may discover new truths about our world—as well as a fresh and unmistakable inspiration for a new way to live.

3

This Is My Father's World

THIS IS MY FATHER'S WORLD

This is my Father's world,

And to my listening ears

All nature sings, and round me rings

The music of the spheres.

This is my Father's world:

I rest me in the thought

Of rocks and trees, of skies and seas;

His hand the wonders wrought.

—MALTBIE BABCOCK

n my college years, studying landscape architecture at Cal Poly Pomona in the early 1980s, I learned to design outdoor areas that are aesthetically pleasing and that work well for their intended uses. One professor in particular—Francis Dean—challenged me to go beyond the exterior aesthetics and consider how designs could work as part of natural systems and processes around them. Professor Dean expected all his students to think beyond simple physical beauty. He inspired us to try for contributions to society that would have more significance than merely beautiful plazas or parks. As a result, he pushed me to consider how I might create places that were both beautiful and environmentally beneficial.

From the start, we had heated discussions. I told him that as a Christian I didn't have much hope that we could have a real impact on the wholesale degradation of the planet. Without faith, I insisted, greed will inevitably cause us to be more concerned with the short term than the long term. Yet he disagreed and remained an optimistic visionary, saying that it didn't matter what others might do and always posing the question, "But what can *you* do to make things better, Mike?"

Looking back, I can see very clearly that this was where my journey to faith truly began. And as I grew, I found truth becoming much more important. I believe some things are inherently true and others are false. My goal is to hold to that which is true. I'm to love my wife and kids sacrificially. I'll reap what I sow. I must avoid lying, cheating, or becoming too impressed with myself. I should not worry about treasures here on earth. I began to realize that my opinions about the environment needed to be grounded in the truths declared by my faith. So I began looking into the Bible for an answer to my question.

What is our responsibility to creation? Over the years, I found five biblical themes that have transformed my outlook and my life.

Theme One: What God Made Is Good

Millions of words have been spilled across thousands of pages to describe how we should relate to God. Our shelves are also brimming with books on how to interact with other people. But comparatively little has been written on how we should relate to the environment. From mountain peaks to the ocean floor, from the most complex animal to the most primitive, from the tallest tree to the most humble rock, how should we view and treat the world around us? Though not commonly discussed in contemporary Christianity, the Bible is not silent about this subject.

In the creation account of Genesis, God Himself paid tribute to the wonder of creation: first light; then sky; then earth; then plants; then sun, moon and stars; then birds and fish, terrestrial animals, and finally man and woman. At every step, God looked at what He had created and declared, "It is *good*." It doesn't quite translate, but the original Hebrew word there is closer in meaning to "inarguably perfect in every way." In fact, when He was completely finished, God looked again at the sum total of all He had made and said "it is *very* good." It wasn't just inarguably perfect; every quality about it was *extremely* perfect.

Any discussion of how our faith interacts with our attitudes about the environment must begin here. God saw that the created world, *all of it*—from slugs to salmon to donkeys and mushrooms and millipedes—was *ridiculously* awesome. And it wasn't just the individual species that God said were very good. The entire planet is the ultimate example of the whole being far greater than the sum of its parts. As interesting a creature as the black rhinoceros is, it's even more fascinating to discover the minuscule helper—termites—it uses to fight off parasitic ticks.

Our world is full of such surprising interrelationships in an incredibly intricate and nonrepeating pattern of complexity. The former analogy of a "food chain" has been more aptly re-termed "the web of life," where the success or failure of an individual organism affects many others. Individual species are sustained by and responsible for countless other species within the context of their particular climates and geographies. Everything is designed to be in precise harmony with its local environment. The more I study the vast wonders of this natural interlocking system, the more I'm amazed by God. He didn't simply call for casting individual species and create separate environments for them all. He scripted an incredible living drama of interaction, dependence, and interdependence upon interdependence. It is the *performance* of this creation in motion that is so ridiculously awesome. How can I not be driven, compelled, obsessed by making sure that this drama will continue to play out just as incredibly for my descendants?

God declared that nature is good, that it has an intrinsic, irreducible value. Nearly fifty years ago, Francis Schaeffer said in *Pollution and the Death of Man,* "It is the biblical view of nature that gives nature a value in itself...because God made it."

Have you ever been the beneficiary of someone's goodness? Has a stranger ever changed a flat tire for you? Has a relative bailed you out of a financial bind, or has a friend kept you from making a grave mistake? After you recognized their selfless acts, were you motivated to insult them, ignore them, or injure them? Probably not. Likewise, if we recognize the true *good*ness endowed in creation by the Creator, how can we not be impelled to appreciate, respect, and protect it as His wonderful gift to us?

God made the world and said it is good. Our response to it should be on par with its great value.

Theme Two: God Loves the World He Created

If we truly love God, we will cherish the things that are valuable to Him. And there can be no biblical doubt that He loves the creation.

Consider this: what is your most prized possession? Picture that item now as we read one of the most famous verses in the New Testament, one that has something to say about God's most precious possession: "For God so loved the world that he gave his one and only Son" (John 3:16).

We tend to read this as "for God so loved *the people* of the world." Surely God was concerned with saving spiritual souls, not the physical reality.

Of course, people were his crowning creation, the last and greatest of his handiworks. But God also expressed his goodness, grace, and power through the totality of his creation. Jesus said He cared about sparrows. The psalmist said that God preserves both man and animals, even that God is "loving toward all he has made" (Psalm 145:17).

Mountaintops can bring that home, perhaps like no other place on earth. Recently, my nephew Ross, son-in-law Chris, and I climbed Mount Hood in the Oregon Cascades. It's not a terribly dangerous climb, but plenty taxing if you've passed your first half-century as I have. Reaching the summit at sunrise, I turned to look across the incredible landscape spread out before us from atop the lip of a volcanic peak at 11,249 feet. Not a cloud in the sky, the view seemed endless in all directions. From there, I felt I was seeing the world that God loved as He saw it every day. As I turned my back on the unveiling sun, an incredible surprise met my eyes. The shadow of the great mountain darkened the sky beneath us. A perfect conical replica of Mount Hood appeared in the early morning moisture-laden air, and I thought to myself, "Can God not put exclamation points in the sky at the dawn of a new day?"

As we know, God has a habit of meeting people on mountaintops. Isn't it at least in part because they make such ideal places to view His world as He does?

Theme Three: What God Made Is God's, *Not* Ours

The concept of ownership is woven throughout the fabric of our culture. We *own* our homes, our property, our independence, our issues. We buy in, sell out, and own up.

So to rouse us from our self-absorbed stupor, the Old Testament speaks a powerful truth: the world is not actually ours. The Creator retains all rights and privileges to His ownership of creation. Not only does he value it, He owns it! In the words of the giant-killer who became the poet-king nearly 2,500 years ago,

> The earth is the LORD's, and everything in it,
>   the world, and all who live in it;
> for he founded it upon the seas
>   and established it upon the waters. (Psalm 24:1–2)

33

And long before David wrote that psalm, God asked of Job:

"Who has a claim against me that I must pay?
Everything under heaven belongs to me." (Job 41:11)

That's pretty clear. But the New Testament gets more specific. Here we learn that all things were created by Jesus, for Jesus. He actually holds everything in the universe together, and by allowing Himself to be sacrificed, Jesus made it possible for everything—people, plants, critters, atmosphere, geology, oceans, all of it—to be reconciled and brought into harmony with God.

For by Him all things were created, both in the heavens and on earth, visible and invisible.... And through Him to reconcile all things to Himself, having made peace through the blood of His cross; through Him, I say, whether things on earth or things in heaven." (Colossians 1:16, 20, NASB)

It reminds me of the joke of a scientist challenging God to a man-making contest to see who can create the best human. As the scientist bends down to scoop up a handful of dirt, God says, "No, no. Get your own dirt." When asked to show proof of our ownership of the world, we reach into our pockets and find nothing but lint. Everything we have belongs to the Creator. Yet rather than seeing ourselves as the stewards of the planet on behalf of the owner, we often treat it as though it is ours to do with as we like. We may not be brazen enough to claim personal title, but our actions tell how we really feel.

This was an important concept for me. Vicki and I live in a house along Fairview Creek in Oregon. I love to sit on my back deck and watch nature around me: the creek flowing around the rise we call the island, the pair of ducks submarining for grubs, the finches and chickadees taking their turns at the feeder, the squirrels competing to get to the corncob, the great blue heron silently stalking fish. I even enjoy spending a day in the creek pulling out the cursed Himalayan blackberry canes.[1]

Vicki and I love our house and enjoy sharing it with family and friends. I know that even though we'll pay off the mortgage someday, we'll never really be the owners. This place, like everywhere else on this earth, is God's. And as temporary tenants, we work for the Landlord, which leads directly to the fourth theme.

Theme Four: Everything Was Created to Glorify God

Closely tied to the concept of ownership is *significance*. Why did God create all this? Why not just leave well enough alone? Why is there not *nothing*? As theologians have wrestled with this over the millennia, one compelling answer has popped up over and over again. It's also woven throughout the Old and New Testaments: we are here, in fact, to bring glory to the Creator.

Because we're part of creation, this is our job. The sun and stars, coral reefs, fungi, salamanders, manatees, and probably even the Himalayan blackberry were created primarily for this purpose: to commend, exalt, and give thanks to God. In His unfathomable wisdom, God

---

1. I realize many might find it hypocritical of me to hate the Himalayan blackberry, or at least to object that the kudzu or Scotch broom is far more evil. But let me assure you, here in the Pacific Northwest, the Himalayan blackberry is the botanical manifestation of Satan—seductive with its juicy berries but laden with thorns that thirst for blood, and more prodigious than a dozen mating rabbits. The man who brought this scourge over from western Europe should have been imprisoned in a cell of thorny canes. But I digress.

designed everything in this universe to all work together in immeasurable complexity so that it could relentlessly glorify Him. As odd as this may sound, it is not just humans that are expected to recognize God's power, wisdom, and love. Everything He created is intended to join in the chorus:

> Praise the LORD, you his angels,
>> you mighty ones who do his bidding,
>> who obey his word.
> Praise the LORD, all his heavenly hosts,
>> you his servants who do his will.
> Praise the LORD, *all his works*
>> *everywhere* in his dominion.

> Praise the LORD, O my soul. (Psalm 103:20–22)

> My mouth will speak in praise of the LORD.
>> Let *every creature* praise his holy name
>> for ever and ever. (Psalm 145:21)

No one is quite sure what it looks like when all His works praise Him. I needed a few more word pictures to help me visualize this. So when I looked further, I found some spectacular imagery:

> The mountains and hills
>> will burst into song before you,
> and all the trees of the field
>> will clap their hands.
> Instead of the thornbush will grow the pine tree,
>> and instead of briers the myrtle will grow.

This will be for the LORD's renown,

    for an everlasting sign,

    which will not be destroyed. (Isaiah 55:12–13)

Let the heavens rejoice, let the earth be glad;

    let the sea resound, and all that is in it;

    let the fields be jubilant, and everything in them.

Then all the trees of the forest will sing for joy;

    they will sing before the LORD, for he comes,

    he comes to judge the earth. (Psalm 96:11–13)

37

Clearly, creation is not a static, worn-out holding cell. The very glory of God is somehow imbedded and infused in the creation and creatures around us.

The more I thought of this, the more it dawned on me that every plant and animal is significant. After all, there are no accidents with God. He purposely thought the world needed these creatures. Who am I to disagree or diminish their importance? And if this is what God has ordained for His created world, what happens if some creature that was designed to praise Him is wiped off the face of the earth? How can a red-legged frog or a gorilla or a spotted owl fulfill its calling if our carelessness or indifference has caused its species to go extinct? Are we responsible for God being less honored, less glorified, less praised?

Theme Five: God Appointed Us Stewards

If we don't own the house or the property where we live, God allows us to live here as a privilege for taking care of it. I'm only one of the many people who have shared responsibility to steward the tiny piece of creation under my care today. My goal is to leave it in better shape than I found it and inspire the next person to accept the mantle of stewardship when it's his or her turn to take up the heavy job of keeping the blackberries out of the creek.

Of course, our responsibility isn't limited to the specific places we inhabit. We're stewards of the entire planet! This was the responsibility given to the first humans, of whom we are the biological and spiritual descendants—the first gardeners of Eden:

Then the LORD God planted a garden in Eden, in the east.…
The LORD God placed the man in the Garden of Eden to tend
and care for it. (Genesis 2:8,15, NLT)

That's right. After he created the world, all the living things, and man, God invented *landscape architecture.* He planted a special, protected garden and added all sorts of beautiful trees and a river to water it. It was probably a purely delightful place, lacking nothing but a gardener. I can see groundskeeper Adam arriving on the scene with his handcrafted trowel and shears—and no tool belt to hang them on. God gave him a job, two tasks, in fact: "to tend" and "care for" the garden. *To tend* can be translated "to work," "to cultivate," "to dress," and "to till." The idea was for Adam to encourage the garden to flourish and reach its full potential. Sounds a little like parenting to me. We encourage, invest in, and support when we tend our kids.

Care for can be translated as "keep." The image in the ancient Hebrew evokes the efforts of shepherds to protect their flocks against predators at night. They would build a protective hedge around a small pasture area sufficient to keep intruders out and sheep in. The shepherd would guard and watch all night, alert to any threats.

Realize that this job was given to Adam before Eve was created, before the whole apple incident. While the world was still pure and sinless, there was meaningful work to be done in this special garden to ensure its health. Gardening Eden was not Adam's punishment; it was his *purpose.*

After God had placed Adam in the garden and created Eve to help in the gardening, He blessed them and gave them these famous instructions:

> Be fruitful and multiply; fill the earth and subdue it; have domin-
> ion over the fish of the sea, over the birds of the air, and over
> every living thing that moves on the earth. (Genesis 1:28, NKJV)

This verse is a key passage—and unfortunately, it's been widely misconstrued, often by those who would paint Christianity as anti-conservation. That word *dominion* implies a position of authority—but authority along with the attendant responsibility. Again, the parent-child dynamic is a helpful analogy. The dominion a parent exercises over a child is obviously one of concern for the long-term best interests of the child. Mothers are to make decisions that nurture and protect their children while allowing them to develop and flourish. This is the "authority-with-responsibility" we're to exercise over creation. An abusive, heavy-handed, dictatorial, or neglectful parent is not exercising dominion.

The humble shepherd and poet David brings this concept into razor-sharp focus with an understanding of the connection between the spiritual and physical worlds:

> When I look at the night sky and see the work of your fingers—
> the moon and the stars you have set in place—
> what are mortals that you should think of us,
> mere humans that you should care for us?

For you made us only a little lower than God,
  and you crowned us with glory and honor.
You put us in charge of everything you made,
  giving us authority over all things—
the sheep and the cattle
  and all the wild animals,
the birds in the sky, the fish in the sea,
  and everything that swims the ocean currents.

O LORD, our Lord, the majesty of your name fills the earth!
(Psalm 8:3–9, NLT)

Along with Adam, we were created to be gardeners of Eden. This is the critical concept of stewardship that helps me understand my true job responsibilities from God. Webster's dictionary defines *stewardship* as "the careful and responsible management of something entrusted to one's care."

Imagine that a million dollars drops out of the sky and lands in the middle of your neighborhood street. Two options race through your mind. You could call all your neighbors, gather up the cash together, and develop a joint investment plan. On the other hand, you could sneak outside unnoticed and pick up all the money for yourself. You have little incentive to work in concert with your neighbors—after all, you'll end up with less than if you just go get it for yourself.

But what if, shortly after the money lands, a limousine pulls into your neighborhood, and out steps a bespectacled attorney. The attorney explains that his boss intentionally dropped the money into your neighborhood. You and your neighbors are to split it equally and ensure that it meets the needs of everyone in the neighborhood. If you choose to just take your share, when the money runs out, that will be the end of it. Alternatively, you and your fellow neighbors can pool the money and invest it wisely, which would result in a trust fund that will meet your current needs as well as those of future generations of neighbors. But for this to work, you and your neighbors will need to pay attention to your lifestyles and live within your means. Are you willing to sacrifice a little now for the benefit of the long term and those who follow after you? Are you willing to be a steward of the money?

Most of us would be tempted to take the money and run. But the Owner doesn't give us this option.

Jesus addressed stewardship in several parables. In Luke 12 he tells of two servants, or stewards. The first one is a faithful steward who maintains the house well when his master goes away. He is ready at all times for the master's return. Certainly an example to follow. The second steward thinks that since the master is gone, he can abandon his responsibilities. When the master returns unexpectedly and finds the negligent steward, the servant is punished severely, because he knew his duty and refused to fulfill it.

God gives us this universe freely, wanting us to discover the joys of responsible stewardship, of moderation, and the freedom that comes with self-discipline and caring for a flock, of not squandering resources. And by doing these things, God tells us, we'll better understand and appreciate Him. He alone knows the deep joy and satisfaction that will be ours when He catches us fulfilling our calling and says to us, "Well done, good and faithful servant!" (Matthew 25:21). It will be unlike anything on this earth—a joy so deep and profound that it will explode our former concept of joy.

People of faith must devote themselves to caring for this planet before it's too late. The creation is very good and in need of protection. God loves it, and we are not its owners. Its purpose, like ours, is to bring glory to the Creator.

God created this intricate world to delight Him, and He created us to make it flourish.

He also gave us one more thing—to remind us of Him and the reason for this responsibility, something that sets us apart from all other creatures.

4

Beauty for the Beast

What words can describe the myriad beauties
of land and sea and sky? Just think of the
illimitable abundance and the marvelous
loveliness of light, or of the beauty of the sun
and moon and stars, of shadowy glades in the
woods and of the color and perfume of flowers,
of the songs and plumage of so many varieties
of birds, of the innumerable animals of every
species that amaze us most when they are
smallest in size. Or take a look at the grandiose
spectacle of the open sea, clothing and
reclothing itself in dresses of changing shades
of green, purple and blue.

—SAINT AUGUSTINE OF HIPPO,
The City of God

Everybody needs beauty as well as bread, places to play in and pray in, where Nature may heal and cheer and give strength to body and soul alike.

—JOHN MUIR, *The Yosemite*

The perception of beauty is a moral test.

—HENRY DAVID THOREAU, *Journal*

The sky was crystal clear, a cobalt blue that could take your breath away. Or perhaps it was the altitude; after all, this was the Colorado Rockies. Beginning at an elevation of 10,000 feet, my lowlander's body pleaded for oxygen as I left Maroon Lake and headed up the steep trail. At the same time, a sense of euphoria carried me rapidly upward. I couldn't get enough of the incredible scenery wrapping 360 degrees around me. The glacier-carved canyon I traversed presented incredible views of two fourteeners, North and South Maroon Peaks. With the aspen trees glowing iridescent gold in the morning light, the scene itself stole my breath away. All my senses were enhanced, and I could virtually *taste* the gorgeous scene, *feel* my skin absorbing it, and *smell* the perfumed mountains.

And then I *heard* the voice of God.

Mike, you're moved by beauty because you're formed in My image. You're happiest when you're experiencing beauty. I made you this way because it's the way I am. I made this earth to please My eye—and yours. Only humans have this appreciation. It's My thumbprint of supernaturalness on you. Your desire for beauty demonstrates My existence.

The "sound" was like an immediate awareness that sprang into my mind.

You're like Me in this way, but also another—you're a creative being. You'll never be more fulfilled than when you're creating something new. Because I'm creative, I gave you this element of Me too. All people, always, everywhere, experience profound satisfaction when they help create something new—no matter what it is. That creativity also demonstrates Me.

The "voice" grew silent, and I soon hiked on, pondering what I'd heard. Later I returned down the trail, but in many ways, I've never left that mountaintop.

Those thoughts coursing through my mind that day were set into motion by sensory overload. I believe that in the thin air I heard something I already knew, but it became clearer to me up there in the Maroon Bells. The prophet Elijah heard God's whisper in much the same way on top of a mountain, though unlike me, God's whisper to Elijah was preceded by a shattering wind, earthquake, and fire!

Back at sea level, the question continues to surface—what is beauty? And why is it so important to us? Of what real, lasting, tangible value is it? Why does a particular scene, person, poem, or piece of music move us so? What is it about us that can explain this aesthetic appreciation? A friend and noted nature photographer, John MacMurray, put it this way:

> We alone, from among all the creatures on this planet, view nature with an appreciation for its beauty. We are interested in nature not only in a functional sense, as all other creatures are, but in an aesthetic sense as well. And this, as far as I can tell, is universal among the human species.[1]

1. John MacMurray, *The Call of Creation* (Eagle Creek, OR: Creation Calendars, 2005), 10.

MacMurray's words capture one of the great, shared experiences of the human race. Across cultures, nationalities, economic conditions, and millennia of time, we have all experienced the sense of awe that "takes our breath away." The noted naturalist John Muir built an entire life and philosophy on an unrelenting quest for this experience. He was fueled by the power that nature's physical beauty has deep in the heart and soul of a person. Recalling his first encounter with the mountains of the Sierra Nevada many years earlier, he mused:

> Bathed in such beauty, watching the expressions ever varying
> on the faces of the mountains, watching the stars, which here
> have a glory that the lowlander never dreams of, watching the
> circling seasons, listening to the songs of the waters and winds
> and birds, would be endless pleasure.... No other place has
> ever so overwhelmingly attracted me as this hospitable, Godful
> wilderness.[2]

47

Though overwhelmingly attractive, beauty is completely unnecessary. Unless, of course, you ever find yourself in need of a little inspiration.

I was in this situation not too long ago. I woke up early in unfamiliar territory. After rolling out of bed, I slid into shorts, T-shirt, and hiking shoes, grabbed a water bottle, and headed out. The morning had dawned predictably bright, with a crystal clarity common in the Sangre de Cristo Mountains of New Mexico. On temporary hiatus from the rainy Pacific Northwest, I breathed deeply the air laced with

---

2. John Muir, *My First Summer in the Sierra* (New York: Houghton Mifflin, 1911), 286–87, 324.

pine and sunbeams. Away from the conference center I hiked, with my eye on a deep red bluff poised above the little valley.

Finding a footpath, I scrambled up out of the valley, through a landscape quieted in the cool of the morning. After an energetic climb of just a few minutes, I emerged from the trees on a broad terrace. Walking forward, I discovered a broad sandstone ledge, gleaming in the early morning and seemingly designed as a perfect perch above the little valley. I welcomed the opportunity to catch my breath as I plopped myself down and savored it all.

This was a time of turmoil for me. I was considering a huge career shift—leaving the company I had started to become a city bureaucrat. In addition, I was trying to do something I had never done before—write a book. Surrounded by professionals and accomplished people, I felt out of my league. Worries about the future, fear of failure and the unknown, had been my recent companions. I needed a little peace and inspiration.

In some miraculous way that defies words or understanding, the Creator of the universe knew my state, my needs, my fears. As I talked to Him from that red rock bluff, my eyes were filled with the incredible contrasts of mountains and valley, rocks and trees. As I gazed at gleaming rocks like sun-struck rubies and felt the sun's warmth on my skin, peacefulness flooded over me. Hadn't God guided my career steps over the past quarter century? Had He not blessed me with an incredible family and devoted friends? Had He not provided the right people at the right time to encourage me in this new adventure? And wasn't the opportunity to be in this stunning place proof that He wanted to share His beauty with me? My anxieties began to melt away.

As I headed back down the hill, I was buoyed by the knowledge that regardless of what was to transpire in my life, I was not alone, and that I had just encountered the Creator again through His creation.

Our quest for beauty makes no ecological sense, and yet it is undeniably real. Though it appears completely unnecessary, all humans insist on it. For some unknowable reason, it's absolutely necessary.

God made the world drop-dead gorgeous. Parts of it, places we haven't defiled, are absolutely stunning. Surprisingly, God didn't choose to keep this creative ability all to Himself. He passed it on to His children. One of the strongest proofs that we are made in His image is that we, too, have been endowed with the ability to create beauty in this world. However, beauty is not limited to the naturally occurring aspects of creation. Ancients described the city of Jerusalem as "the perfection of beauty" (Lamentations 2:15). Even places where human hands have touched skillfully, like Italian hill towns, well-kept farms, or large architectural structures can carry a beauty all their own.

Artists and designers are fortunate enough to turn this inner drive into something others can appreciate. As a landscape architect, I have experienced the fulfilling joy that comes with creating something beautiful. The joy I feel when I see children playing or people relaxing in a park I've designed, appreciating a garden, hiking through a restored wetland, or even strolling down a unique shopping street helps me understand the love the Creator feels toward His creation.

Unlike a painter, I have a palette of man-made materials such as concrete and brick; natural materials such as plants, rock, and wood; and the elements of light and water.[3] Your palette is likely different. You may express your creativity by inventing a new recipe, restoring an old

---

3. The added element of time, by the way, is one major difference between architects and landscape architects. A building never looks better than the day it is opened, but a good landscape never looks worse than on that day. A landscape needs time to grow and become the place the designer imagined.

car, writing a poem, or designing your own home. The list of ways we humans practice creative expression is almost limitless.

This drive to create something beautiful is undeniably universal among us. It may be one of the defining characteristics of humanity. A tree doesn't merely provide habitat for living creatures; it serves as inspiration to a poet, an artist, or folks just like you and me. The prophet Ezekiel captured both the ecological and the aesthetic dimensions when he used a tree as a metaphor for the ancient kingdom of Assyria:

> All the birds of the air
>   nested in its boughs,
> all the beasts of the field
>   gave birth under its branches;
> all the great nations
>   lived in its shade.
> It was majestic in beauty,
>   with its spreading boughs,
> for its roots went down
>   to abundant waters....
> I made it beautiful
>   with abundant branches,
> the envy of all the trees of Eden
>   in the garden of God. (Ezekiel 31:6–7, 9)

Ezekiel wasn't just whistling ecology here; he was emotionally moved by the beauty of a great tree. Undoubtedly, he'd had an encounter with a tree like this at some point in his life. His memory and his imagination were at work.

But even if science cannot explain why we are so drawn to beauty, we cannot deny its existence and its benefits.

The Benefits of Beauty

Beyond the inspiration it provides, whether we're looking at a painting by Monet, resting in an alpine meadow, or listening to our favorite music, beauty can transform our minds. In fact, those corporate motivational posters you may have seen are built on this truth. Matched to incredible pictures of nature comes an inspirational thought: "ATTITUDE—your attitude almost always determines your altitude in life." Quick, powerful, inspiration to go.

I am not a big fan of the dentist's office. What with the staff walking around in little white smocks, outdated reading material, and people sitting around with that look of dread in their eyes, it's not my favorite place to hang out. When someone says, "I'd rather get a root canal," you know he or she is facing pretty dire straits.

However, I've noticed that many dentists' offices do have one thing going for them. They often have wonderful photographs of nature scattered about on the walls. Beautiful alpine meadows festooned with wildflowers. Glacial peaks reflected perfectly in remote mountain lakes. Towering redwood trees reaching toward the heavens. Sometimes, I've been surprised to look up from my prone position in the chair and see beautiful natural scenes applied to the ceiling.

So here in this place of oral reconstruction, we find images of nature. Doesn't this seem just a bit incongruous? It is, unless you realize that dentists long ago discovered this basic characteristic of their patients—reflecting on nature gives us a measure of peace and calm. The babbling alpine brook in our imagination drowns out the sound of the drill! We city and town dwellers, accustomed to virtually unlimited creature comforts, on-demand lifestyles, and instant gratification, look outward to find tranquility and serenity. We love the beauty of wild places, even if we never visit them.

This is why Psalm 23 is one of the best-loved scriptures. It offers peace in the midst of turmoil. And it describes the peace and rest it offers in environmental terms:

> He makes me lie down in green pastures,
> he leads me beside quiet waters,
>> he restores my soul. (verses 2–3)

Experiencing beauty can bring us peace, and it can invigorate us as well. Have you ever been driving along and been moved to turn up the volume on a song and start singing? I'm no neurologist, but I'd wager that such auditory beauty prompts powerful chemicals to start flowing and synapses to wake up and begin firing. I know whenever I do this, there's a big, stupid grin on my face, and the speedometer is probably trying to tell me that I'm close to qualifying for a speeding ticket. But I'm just soaring away on a fresh wind of inspiration—a wonderful, unexpected attitude adjustment—and I'm motivated to continue my day with new energy.

Studies do show that all this appreciation of beauty is good for us. In recent years, compelling research has documented the psychological and physiological benefits of nature's beauty. The restorative power of creation calls to us.

Just as dentists have figured out, hospitals and other health-care professionals have become aware of the beneficial effects of the outdoors on the health of patients. Clinical studies have documented that emotional and physical pain levels are lower for patients when they spend time outside the hospital. Even a view of the outdoor world can improve patients' health and shorten their recovery time. This has spawned a movement to incorporate therapeutic gardens and views of nature in the design of health-care facilities. Healing gardens, gardening plots, and outdoor nature paths are now becoming commonplace in senior assisted-living facilities. As one researcher described it, "Seeing the sky or feeling the sun on your skin can literally make you feel better…our surroundings affect our well-being."[4]

But it doesn't take a medical researcher to make the connection between health and nature. A thirteen-year-old girl, hiding in Holland, understood this reality more than sixty years ago:

> The best remedy for those who are frightened, lonely or unhappy is to go outside, somewhere they can be alone, alone with the sky, nature and God. For then and only then can you feel that everything is as it should be and that God wants people to be happy amid nature's beauty and simplicity.
>
> As long as this exists, and that should be forever, I know that there will be solace for every sorrow, whatever the circumstances. I firmly believe that nature can bring comfort to all who suffer.[5]

When we experience beauty in the world around us, we find peace, rest, and improved health. We also find a type of inspiration lacking elsewhere. Perhaps this is one reason God made the world so beautiful: to inspire us in the midst of our difficult daily lives. Beauty also may be God's way of reminding us about the job He gave us—to work it and care for it. It's God's prize for us; a constant reminder of the inescapable fact that life is to be enjoyed for the sheer pleasure of it all. Perhaps there is a supernatural purpose for beauty after all—beauty

---

4. L. Mack, "New Woodbury hospital uses natural ambiance to assist the healing process: Woodwinds is an example of push to make facilities patient friendly," *Minneapolis Star Tribune,* July 30, 2001.
5. Anne Frank, *Anne Frank: the Diary of a Young Girl* (New York: Random House, 1995), 197.

serves as a catalyst for the peace, inspiration, motivation, and joy God wants people to experience.

Yet we often don't see it. Beauty gets overlooked. It's as if we have to be forced to remove the scales of materialism and entertainment from our eyes so that we can see the beauty in the universe God created, the beauty intended to fill us with joy, rest, and inspiration. Beauty is our reward, the ideal to shoot for, the benchmark against which to measure our success or failure. Here is a barometer for us to monitor in ourselves: the extent to which we can recognize and appreciate beauty in our lives may indicate the condition of our spiritual walk with the Creator. The closer we are walking with the Creator, the more beauty we will see in life. As the great thinker Francis Schaeffer said nearly forty years ago:

> So if we did nothing else in our Christian view of nature than
> to save and enjoy beauty, it would be of value, and worth-
> while.... When we have learned this—the Christian view of
> nature—then there can be a real ecology; beauty will flow,
> psychological freedom will come, and the world will cease to
> be turned into a desert.[6]

As the famous sculptor Auguste Rodin remarked, "To the artist there is never anything ugly in nature." When nature is cultivated to flourish in health, it can't be anything other than beautiful.

So acknowledging our calling as stewards of creation is the first step. Being grateful for the blessing of beauty in the world is the second. Step three is to evaluate how we're living up to our calling and blessing as gardeners, which is what we need to look at next.

---

6. Francis Schaeffer, *Pollution and the Death of Man,* (Wheaton, IL: Tyndale, 1970), 93.

5

The Signs of the Times

Because of this the land mourns
and all who live in it waste away;
the beasts of the field and the birds of the air
and the fish of the sea are dying.

—Hosea 4:3

U nfortunately, people are starting to notice many signs indicating that the ideals of stewarding creation and expressing gratitude for natural beauty aren't being respected as well as we might hope.

Here in the Pacific Northwest, it's common to find "idiot strips"—one-hundred-foot-wide perimeters of trees along well-traveled roads that hide clear-cut logging from view. Driving through these corridors, all appears well with the world. But important clues give the truth away: A muddy brown creek. Bright sunlight through the crowns of the trees. But when seen from the air, it's impossible to miss what's nearly invisible at ground level. Behind this roadside fringe of trees, devastation extends up and over the landscape beyond. In classic clear-cut situations near roadways, loggers commonly leave a fringe of trees to conceal the ugliness from the general public and avoid a public outcry. Not coincidentally, public sentiment against clear-cutting has largely coincided with broad access to satellite aerial photography. Once the scales come off our eyes and we're able to see beyond the veneer, we realize how vitally important the beauty of creation truly is to us. When we are faced with these signs of poor stewardship, how can we deny our responsibility?

You reap what you sow. We all understand this elemental truth of life, regardless of how far from a farm we grow up. You don't plant corn and harvest a bushel of boysenberries. We connect the dots between cause and effect. This truth may be self-evident, but it is not exclusively agricultural.

In high school, I lived in the Antelope Valley, a portion of the Mojave Desert about fifty miles north of Los Angeles. I rode motorcycles across the desert, hunted jack rabbits with a .22 rifle, learned to catch lizards and snakes, and didn't think for an instant that the dusty desert around me was a fragile place.

That changed in the summer of 1973. After finding my sophomore biology class more interesting than I expected, I enrolled in a summer-school class called Field Biology, taught by Mike Hanlon, a phenomenal teacher. One hot June morning, I joined eleven of my fellow summer-school students to walk across the street from Palmdale High School to just another undeveloped patch of dusty desert. Mr. Hanlon explained that we were going to do a remarkable thing—we were going to determine the type and number of plants living in one square mile of the desert. He then explained how we were to lay out a ten-foot by ten-foot quadrant and then identify and count everything we found in the quadrant.

For the first time in my life, I looked at nature up close and personal. I learned the difference between a creosote bush and rabbit brush, to be able to tell Joshua trees from Spanish dagger yuccas. I discovered that one way the creosote bush fights off competitors is by creating a water-repellant soil layer beneath its branches. I noticed that in the harsh, inhospitable desert, plants distribute themselves at a fairly low and regular density, leaving plenty of breathing room between neighbors. I dutifully counted up the number of plants living in my quadrant and then consolidated my info with that of my classmates. Multiplying our results, we arrived at the total number of each of these plants that would occur in a square mile of desert.

Mr. Hanlon was not satisfied with this simple numbers game. For the next six weeks, he taught us the interrelationships between the climate, soils, plants, and animals of the desert. We learned that there was a balance between the numbers of chuckwallas, kangaroo rats, and coyotes of the Mojave. He warned us that the desert was being erased by development at a rapid rate and that it could vanish during our lifetimes (a prophecy that has been nearly fulfilled in the thirty-four years since). He helped us understand the impacts we have on the natural world around us and urged us to be citizens who make conscious decisions about the way our society develops. We emerged from his class with a deeper appreciation for the remarkable place where we lived. For the first time, I saw the desert as something valuable that could be lost. I saw that, indeed, we reap what we sow.

The physical world is wonderfully complex, but thankfully predictable. Chaos does not reign. God designed the creation so that we could understand it and predict events, based upon the realities of cause and effect:

- *We all need a home:* populations of animals are affected most directly by reductions or degradation of their habitat. Some of the most life-filled habitat types—wetlands, plains, tropical rain forests, rivers and streams—are the ones most subject to adverse impacts by humans.
- *Creatures are like dominos:* if a certain animal is wiped out, the predators that depend on that species for food will decline, and the plants or animals the animal consumed will likely see their populations explode.

- *Everything flows downhill:* what happens at the upper reaches of a watershed impacts areas hundreds or even thousands of miles downstream.
- *The earth has a lid on it:* if we pump carbon dioxide and other greenhouse gases into the air, sunlight reflecting off the earth's surface will become trapped in the atmosphere and heat up the planet.
- *If you build a house on sand…you are a fool.*

This last reality comes directly from the words of Jesus, who understood how nature works and expects the same of us. A wise person builds a house on solid rock, He said. Only a foolish person builds a house on sand. Why? Jesus described what happened to a house built on sand. "The rain came down, the streams rose, and the winds blew and beat against that house, and it fell with a great crash" (Matthew 7:27). His purpose wasn't to give a scientific explanation of the effects of climate on residential housing. However, He expected His listeners to be students of the natural world around them, including the climate. Since they understood the world around them, Jesus was confident that this analogy would be effective in communicating a deeper, spiritual truth: ignoring His teaching is as foolish as ignoring the natural patterns of weather.

Are we educated stewards of the natural world God created? Do we see and understand what is occurring to the creation in our times? It is difficult to miss the warning signs of environmental degradation that are all around us. Air quality warnings urge us to stay indoors, limit physical activity, and drive only if absolutely necessary. Dire predictions of global warming cause us to wonder if we should ditch our winter coats in favor of Hawaiian shirts and shorts. Long-term droughts culminate in catastrophic fires that destroy homes as well as habitats. Oil spills on distant Arctic shores bring images of tarry-feathered sea birds. Litter comes to rest alongside roads like just so much urban flotsam washed ashore by the waves of passing traffic. Then we open a newspaper, log onto an Internet news site, or turn on the television.

As I write this, a small sampling of recent headlines includes:

"White House Weighing New U.S. CO_2 Proposal"

"Coastal Planners Ready for Sea-Level Rise"

"As Logging Fades, Rich Carve Up Open Land in West"

"Smog Traps California Community"

"Science Panel Says Global Warming Is 'Unequivocal'"

"Low-Level Toxicants Can Harm Brain"

"Orangutans Face 'Emergency,' U.N. Reports"

"Canada Sees Its Greenhouse Gas Emissions Soaring"

"NY to Sue over Slow Cleanup of Oil Slick"

"N.W. China Drought Dries up Water Supplies"

The litany of sobering headlines may convince us to go "shield's up"—to protect our psyche by preventing the bad news from taking up residence in our minds and hearts. Ignorance may not be bliss, but it sure beats having to constantly wrestle with difficult issues and our responsibilities in these matters.

Our Environmental Checking Account

Our desire to avoid bad news reminds me of an embarrassing incident. Not long ago, I was in a period of blinding busyness. I was feeling overwhelmed at work, traveling a lot, and juggling multiple deadlines, as well as responsibilities at church and other commitments. The rubber band was stretched to the breaking point.

At the same time, unexpected financial demands kept cropping up over a period of two or three weeks. You know the kind—a car repair here, a child's school expense there—surprising, but not unwarranted. I had a sense that we were becoming a bit overextended, but I kept telling myself that I would look into our financial standing "tomorrow." If needed, I would transfer funds to make sure our unexpected obligations were taken care of. But of course, my good intentions alone didn't resolve the issue. I needed to act immediately. But I didn't. And you can guess what happened next.

The rubber band snapped.

Letters started to arrive. You know the kind—the ones that feel like you've just been kicked in the gut by a steel-toed boot? By the time I opened the letters and checked the status of the accounts, we were in arrears and accumulating late fees at a supersonic clip. My lack of attention to the immediate challenges of life had put me in a hole that was embarrassing to dig out of. It was a temporary setback and relatively simple to resolve, but it was educational nonetheless. My plight was completely preventable. That is, if I hadn't been so foolish about ordering my priorities.

So it is with the challenges we're facing as stewards of creation today. If one of our responsibilities as human beings is to be the gentle gardeners of the earth, we have to steady ourselves, take a deep breath, and face the realities of our planet's health. We have to honestly investigate the condition of our environmental checking account.

Consider the Source

Once we see our need to acknowledge our personal accountability to the planet, we must become educated about ecological issues. And as we've discussed earlier, oftentimes the most difficult question is not "What should I do?" but rather "Who should I believe?" On some environmental issues, such as global climate change, heavy debate continues, even among evangelicals, as well as among scientists themselves.

Though science can be inconclusive and often misleading, on the whole, scientists are not engaged in an antifaith conspiracy. The collective field of science and research is not out to prove that God does not exist. Even if scientists wanted to, they could not. Faith is not so simple—or fragile.

There are several ironies in the attitude that science is diametrically opposed to issues of faith. If you believe in God, you likely believe in universal, or absolute, truth. Universal truth claims that by its very nature, a truth is true, regardless of the beliefs of the person who discovers or announces it. Scientists can no more disprove a truth than they can create a truth where it doesn't exist. Philosopher Arthur F. Holmes said it this way: "All truth is God's truth." Whether discovered by a rabbi or researcher, skeptic or scientist, if something is true, it must be approved by God.

The skepticism and ridicule Galileo received at the hands of the Catholic church in the 1600s began when he stated that he believed the earth revolved around the sun rather than everything revolving around the earth. Defying the conventional wisdom of the day, he was subjected to vicious criticism and persecution, and the leaders of the church were convinced his theory assaulted the established (universal) truth of the day. However, Galileo understood that if his theory "were proved, then it could not contradict the Scriptures when they were rightly understood."[1] Of course, once Galileo was found to be right, science wasn't wrong, and neither were the Scriptures. But it wasn't until 1992 that Galileo was issued an apology by Pope John Paul II, who himself linked the spiritual and scientific worlds. Science and faith have always had a strained relationship.

There may be a few isolated individuals who see in science the ability to disprove God, but it certainly is not true of the broad scientific community. By their very nature, scientists are professional skeptics. They are reluctant to endorse an idea until there has been an overwhelming preponderance of evidence. Because of this, we should not be surprised when scientists hold wildly different opinions on a range of subjects. However, on the vast majority of environmental issues, both secular and faith-filled scientists are in agreement.

And there are plenty of faith-filled scientists. For nearly one hundred years, the percentage of scientists who believe in a personal God has remained constant at about 40 percent.[2] The American Scientific Affiliation is "A Fellowship of Christians in Science." Its membership consists of thousands "of men and women in science who share a common fidelity to the Word of God and a commitment to integrity in the practice of science."

In his bestseller *The Language of God,* Francis Collins, the brilliant scientist responsible for leading the United States' efforts to decode

---

1. Galileo Galilei, "Letter to the Grand Duchess Christina of Tuscany," 1615.
2. www.asa3.org/asa/newsletter/mayjun07.pdf.

the human genome, affirms the unity of the scientific and spiritual perspectives:

> In this modern era…is there still the possibility of a richly satisfying harmony between the scientific and spiritual world-views? I answer with a resounding *yes!*… Science's domain is to explore nature. God's domain is in the spiritual world, a realm not possible to explore with the tools and language of science. It must be examined with the heart, the mind, and the soul—and the mind must find a way to embrace both realms.[3]

In other words, all truth is God's truth, regardless of its origins—either scientific or spiritual. So what do the seekers and explorers of truth in our natural world have to say about the current state of the planet?

As we know, this amazing planet is a study in interconnectedness. "When we try to pick out anything by itself, we find it hitched to everything else in the universe," wrote John Muir.[4] Any discussion of issues of creation care and environmental stewardship faces this dilemma. How can we talk about individual topics while recognizing they are inextricably linked with others?

For the purposes of clarity, we will look at the current state of the planet in these broad categories:

- air and atmosphere
- oceans
- land and fresh water

3. Francis S. Collins, *The Language of God* (New York: Free Press, 2006), 5–6.
4. John Muir, *My First Summer in the Sierra* (New York: Houghton Mifflin, 1911), 211.

Air and Atmosphere

"He stretches out the heavens like a tent.... And rides
on the wings of the wind." (Psalm 104:2–3)

Is it an accident that this initial feature of creation is the source of so much attention in our times? The heavens—the air and atmosphere—not only contain the breath of life but shield us from the sun's radiation. Atmosphere is an invisible yet life-giving blanket draped over the planet. Herein lie some of the most talked-about environmental issues of our day—global warming and climate change, ozone depletion, air pollution, and acid rain.

Global Warming

We live in a bubble, with the earth's atmosphere as a protective canopy. Much like a greenhouse roof, the atmosphere allows sunlight to pass through to the surface of the earth. The earth's surface can then absorb sunlight so that it's warm enough to support life. However, some of the radiation in the sunlight is reflected off the surface of the planet and heads back to space through the leaky greenhouse roof. There is a delicate balance in the atmosphere that retains just the right amount of heat and lets the rest vanish into space. This is the infamous "greenhouse effect," and we are fortunate it is the way God designed this planet. Without it, we'd be sucking on Popsicles until we froze to death.

If the atmosphere becomes too concentrated with greenhouse gases, it traps too much heat and doesn't allow enough to pass through to space. These greenhouse gases can come from natural sources, such as the oceans, rotting vegetation, or solar flares. However, greenhouse gases such as carbon dioxide are also produced in the burning of petroleum and coal. That's why our cars and power plants are major contributors of carbon into the atmosphere.

I am no climatologist. However, an international panel of several hundred experts—The Intergovernmental Panel on Climate Change (IPCC)—has been looking at this issue since 1988. As I mentioned earlier, it is often difficult to get two scientists to agree on any one topic, so how difficult would it be to get hundreds of scientists from around the world to agree on a topic as complex as global climate change? Remarkably, after researching this issue for nearly twenty years, the IPCC came to consensus on several issues and released the following conclusions in the "IPCC Fourth Assessment Report," released in April and May 2007:

1. Warming of the climate system is unequivocal, evidenced by increases in global air and ocean temperatures, widespread melting of snow and ice, and rising global average sea levels.

2. Evidence for all continents and most oceans indicates that many natural systems are being affected by temperature increases and other climate changes.

3. Global greenhouse gas emissions have grown substantially since pre-industrial times, and increased 70 percent from 1970–2004.

4. Most of the increased temperatures observed since the mid-twentieth century are very likely due to increased greenhouse gas emissions caused by human activity.

If global warming were real, we would expect to see various changes in the earth: glaciers receding, polar icecaps shrinking, and major disruptions in longstanding climate patterns of temperature and rainfall. This, in turn would lead to changes in ocean currents, vegetation

67

patterns and wildlife species. These are exactly the kind of changes that scientists are observing:

- Temperature records for over 150 years show that eleven of the twelve hottest years on record have all occurred in the past twelve years, from 1995–2006. In addition, of the twenty-one hottest years ever measured, twenty have occurred in the last twenty-five years.[5]

- Migratory birds in Europe and North America are changing their schedules, arriving at their northern seasonal homes eight days earlier than normal.[6]

- The Arctic polar icecap, normally ten feet thick, has been steadily decreasing in thickness since 1970. In 2002, the largest ice shelf in the Arctic suddenly cracked in half.[7]

- Glaciers around the world are shrinking and have been since about 1850. The retreat has been rapid since 1990. The shrinking of glaciers has been strongest in Alaska, North America, and Patagonia.[8]

- Population levels of the famous Emperor penguins have dropped 50 to 70 percent in just the last fifty years.

---

5. "IPCC, 2007: Summary for Policymakers," *Climate Change 2007: The Physical Science Basis. Contribution of Working Group I to the Fourth Assessment Report of the Intergovernmental Panel on Climate Change*, ed. S. Solomon et al, (New York: Cambridge University Press, 2007).

6. Peter A. Cotton, "Avian Migration Phenology and Global Climate Change Proceedings of the National Academy of Sciences of the United States of America," September 30, 2003.

7. "Recent Warming of Arctic May Affect Worldwide Climate," NASA, October 23, 2003, www.nasa.gov/centers/goddard/news/topstory/2003/1023esuice.html.

8. P. Lemke, et al, "Changes in Snow, Ice and Frozen Ground." Climate Change 2007: The Physical Science Basis. Contribution of Working Group I to the Fourth Assessment Report of the Intergovernmental Panel on Climate Change (New York: Cambridge University Press, 2007).

Scientists believe that penguin populations are dropping as the coldest food-rich water currents have shifted locations away from the penguin colonies.[9]

- Arctic ice is melting at a rapid rate, and in the summer of 2007, the Arctic ice sheet shrank to the smallest area ever recorded.[10]

- Trees are leafing out earlier in the spring. Oak trees in England leafed out an average of sixteen days earlier in the period 1992 to 1999 than they did forty years earlier in 1952 to 1959.[11]

Most scientists involved with the climate concur that two changes have occurred in the last thirty years: there has been a measurable increase in the average temperatures around the globe, and there has also been a measurable increase in the concentration of greenhouse gases in the atmosphere. This is why so much attention has been given to reducing the amount of carbon dioxide and other greenhouse gases that we release into the atmosphere. Climatologists are urging us to reestablish that delicate balance that allows the proper amount of radiated heat to leave the atmosphere and enter space.

In January 2006, eighty-six evangelical Christian leaders from around the country issued a statement urging believers to take action on the following four claims:

Claim 1: Human-Induced Climate Change Is Real

---

9. John Roach, "Penguin Decline in Antarctica Linked with Climate Change," National Geographic News, May 9, 2001, http://news.nationalgeographic.com/news/2001/05/0509_penguindecline.html; Christophe Barbraud and Henri Weimerskirch, "Penguins and Climate Change," Nature 411, *International Weekly Journal of Science*, May 2001.

10. Fiona Harvey, "Nearing Meltdown," *Financial Times,* May 30, 2008.

11. "Review of UK Climate Change Indicators," Department for Environment Food and Rural Affairs, United Kingdom, Revised January 2004. www.ecn.ac.uk/iccuk/.

Claim 2: The Consequences of Climate Change Will Be Significant, and Will Hit the Poor the Hardest

Claim 3: Christian Moral Convictions Demand Our Response
to the Climate Change Problem

Claim 4: The Need to Act Now Is Urgent

The list of signatories to "Climate Change: An Evangelical Call to
Action"[12] was quite diverse, and included the Rev. Dr. Rick Warren,
pastor and author of *The Purpose Driven Life;* Richard Stearns, president of World Vision; Dr. Duane Litfin, president of Wheaton College;
Bill Hybels, pastor of Willow Creek Community Church in Chicago;
and Rev. Jack Hayford, president of the International Church of the
Foursquare Gospel in Los Angeles. These and other men and women
of faith looked at the evidence and the tenets of Scripture and were
convinced that we should act now.

However, consensus is not unanimous. Although many scientists
agree that we are experiencing measurable climate change, the role that
human activity has played in this phenomena has caused vigorous
debates. A small but notable minority of climate scientists believe that
the cause of global warming has been an increase in solar activity rather
than human activity. They suggest that sunspots and solar flares have
long been linked to rapid changes in temperatures here on earth.

A few of their primary arguments include:

- Global climate and temperatures have always fluctuated.
- Increased CO_2 levels are an effect, not a cause, of global
climate warming.
- Even if CO_2 is significant in global warming, humans are
minimally responsible.

---

12. Evangelical Climate Initiative, www.christiansandclimate.org/statement.

- There is little direct evidence that human activity has an effect on global climate.

So what's a gardener of Eden to do? Go back to the beginning. We're to be faithful stewards of creation.

Even if global warming skeptics are correct and human activity is not causing global warming, are we absolved from worrying about burning fossil fuels and increasing CO_2 in the atmosphere? Think about some other consequences of our dependence on burning coal, oil, and gas as our primary sources of energy. The environmental impacts include:

- Drilling, transporting, and refining oil (remember the Exxon Valdez oil spill and the deadly explosion at BP's Texas City refinery?)
- Smog and other types of air pollution, which cause human health problems
- Exhaustion of a finite energy resource we may need for more important future priorities
- Global conflicts over access to diminishing oil resources

Regardless of the CO_2-global warming argument, it's likely that the earth and its inhabitants would be better off if we used less coal, oil, and fossil fuels. Not only that, our appreciation of creation would be stronger if we could actually see the mountains that God created, rather than having them obscured by smog or removed by mountaintop-removal coal mining.

Ozone Depletion

Ozone is a naturally occurring substance that functions in our atmosphere like the earth's sunscreen. Even in very low concentrations six to thirty miles above the earth's surface, ozone molecules block harmful ultraviolet rays from the sun. This is very important to life on earth and particularly human health, as ultraviolet radiation is a known cause of skin cancer, glaucoma, and other maladies. One could say that without ozone, we're toast!

Unfortunately, our society created a number of chemicals that destroy these ozone molecules. For more than fifty years, we released chlorofluorocarbons (CFCs) into the air without knowing their effect. In the 1970s, scientists discovered that CFCs break down in the stratosphere and release chlorine. One chlorine molecule can destroy over 100,000 ozone molecules. Since there are only three ozone molecules for every 2 million oxygen molecules in the air, ozone is too precious to destroy.

The depletion of ozone in the atmosphere has occurred around the entire world, but it has been most severe above Antarctica. Here the so-called "hole in the ozone layer" has developed. The "hole" is actually an area of very low concentrations of ozone, well below the level needed to adequately prevent ultraviolet radiation from reaching the earth's surface. Getting a suntan in Antarctica is not recommended.

The world community reacted quickly and with surprising unity to this global environmental problem. Since 1987 when the Montreal Protocol was initially drafted, 193 countries, including the United States, agreed to completely end the production of the most harmful CFCs by 1996.

Because of these swift measures, emissions of ozone-depleting substances have dropped dramatically. However, CFCs and chlorine persist a long time in the stratosphere. In September 2006, National Aeronautics and Space Administration (NASA) and National Oceanic and Atmospheric Administration (NOAA) measured the largest hole in the ozone layer ever recorded—10.6 million square miles. In spite of this, scientists expect that the ozone layer will rebuild itself gradually over the next fifty years as long as we do not release additional CFCs or other chlorine-producing emissions into the atmosphere.

Air Pollution and Acid Rain

There is both good news and bad news here. Air pollution in the United States has been declining over the past three decades as we put tougher regulations and requirements in place. There are fewer days when school children are asked to remain indoors. Since 1980, four of the primary pollutants monitored by the Environmental Protection Agency have been reduced by half. Yet, even with this significant improvement, about 140 million tons of pollutants are released to the atmosphere each year in the United States.[13] This results in over 120 million people living in areas that have levels of harmful pollutants higher than the government's air quality standards. Though the city of Los Angeles has reduced its number of poor-air-quality days to about one a year, the nearby San Joaquin Valley town of Arvin averages seventy-three poor-air-quality days a year, with a rate of asthma in children 44 percent greater than the national average.[14] And that's the good news.

It is much bleaker in other places around the world. In developing countries, air pollution levels are increasing at rates far outpacing improvements we are making in North America. Areas of China, India, Korea, and Mexico have some of the worst air quality in the world. The World Health Organization has estimated that two million people a year are killed by outdoor air pollution and another 1.6 million from air pollution indoors.

---

13. "Latest Findings on National Air Quality," U.S. Environmental Protection Agency, January 2008.
14. Sonya Geis, "Smog Traps California Community," *Washington Post*, October 8, 2007.

Unfortunately, air pollution doesn't recognize national borders. The front page of the Oregonian newspaper in March 2007 announced: "China's Dirty Air Threatens Darker Days for Northwest." The article discussed black carbon soot from China's industrial plants drifting across the Pacific Ocean and reaching the west coast of North America. Some scientists believe that, in addition to decreasing our air quality, China's thickening air pollution has been the primary cause of the dramatic increase of rainfall along the Pacific Northwest coast over the past ten years.

74

"Acid rain" describes a phenomenon where airborne pollutants, primarily sulfur dioxide and nitrogen oxide, combine with water in the atmosphere to form mild sulfuric or nitric acid. The primary sources of these pollutants are automobile exhaust and petroleum- and coal-fired power plants. Winds transport the acids and later deposit them on the trees, plants, or freshwater streams and lakes on the ground. These pollutants can travel hundreds of miles before they descend. When they land, they change the chemistry of the water and soil they land on, affecting many plant and animal species. The effects of acid rain on amphibians, fish, plants, and entire forests can range from stunted growth to widespread death, depending on the severity and duration of the exposure. This is a major issue of concern in the northeast United States, Canada, and Europe. Since scientists first identified acid rain in the 1970s, substantial improvements have occurred. However, the current rapid growth of Asian economies and industries threatens to reverse recent gains elsewhere in the world.

Air pollution and acid rain illustrate how our global interdependence has ecologic as well as economic implications. We are just starting to recognize the environmental impacts of the United States' market for cheap goods produced in Asia. It's time we began to reevaluate our demand for these goods and encourage our government to advocate for more stringent environmental protection measures around the world, starting here at home.

In summary, our areas of progress in the stewardship of air and atmosphere are not keeping up with the pace of new and expanding sources of pollution. The bottom line is this: people are dying because of poor air quality, and humans have the ability to prevent these deaths. But do we have the will?

Oceans

"There is the sea, vast and spacious, teeming with creatures beyond number." (Psalm 104:25)

Think for a moment about what a fascinating place exists beneath the curtain of the ocean's surface. Coral reefs, kelp forests, tropical lagoons, and underwater dunes all invite us to strap on scuba gear and explore. The number of incredible creatures found there is truly endless; we have no idea of all the species that exist in the ocean's depths. Jellyfish, humpback whales, sea turtles, great white sharks, electric eels, sea horses, octopuses, and manta rays are just a few.

The oceans, like the atmosphere above our heads, are vitally important, but few of us think about them on a regular basis. I used to think about the ocean quite a bit when I was in the navy aboard the USS *Gridley* in the late 1970s. I loved going to sea. It was a thrill every time we sailed from port in San Diego and felt the first rising ocean swells as we passed Buoy 1SD. I always loved the seals, whales, and flying fish we spotted at sea.

As farmers have a deep appreciation for the land, those involved in the coastal fishing industry are astute students of ocean health. Pietro

Parravano, a coastal fisherman in Half Moon Bay, California, and appointed to the Pew Oceans Commission, described it this way:

> Certainly if you look at the ground fish disasters in New England and the Pacific Coast, the status of most shark populations and some other fisheries, one could easily conclude we have a disaster at hand and radical change is needed.
>
> My colleagues and I became fishermen because we love working on the water and we love feeding people.... Fishermen possess a great deal of knowledge about the ocean and its fish that has accumulated over generations.... Fishermen continually tell us that the most important thing we can do for our industry is protect habitat. Fishermen know that better than anyone.... This is why fishermen are every bit as concerned with coastal development that limits our access to the oceans, polluted runoff that chokes coastal waters, and introduced species that disrupt ecosystem functions as we are with...fishery management reform.[15]

Recognizing an impending environmental crisis, Congress passed the Oceans Act of 2000, declaring the importance of oceans to the ecologic, economic, and cultural future of the country. President George W. Bush then appointed sixteen members to the Commission on Ocean Policy. Some of the findings the commission included in its 2004 final report include:

---

15. "Our Nation's Oceans: Looking Ahead. A Perspective from America's Oldest Industry," Pietro Parravano, speaking for the Pacific Coast Federation of Fisher-men's Association on April 19, 2002, to the U.S. Commission on Ocean Policy, www.oceancommission .gov/meetings/apr18_19_02/parravano_testimony.pdf.

- The ocean is important to our economy.

Ten percent of the U.S. annual gross domestic product is generated in the narrow near-shore area along the coast of the United States. If we expand the zone to include the complete economies of all coastal counties, the impact swells to half of our entire GDP.

- Coastal areas are growing.

More than half of the U.S. population lives in coastal counties. In the past thirty years, nearly 40 million people have moved into coastal areas, driving up real estate values and causing significant environmental impacts.

- Coastal areas are not healthy.

In 2001, nearly one-fourth of the coastal areas were deemed impaired for swimming, fishing, or marine life. Experts estimate that globally, 25 to 30 percent of ocean fish stocks are overexploited. Since the United States was founded, nearly half of all fresh and saltwater wetlands have been destroyed.

Reporting to a conservative Congress and president, the commission summarized its findings:

> Our failure to properly manage the human activities that affect
> the nation's oceans, coasts, and Great Lakes is compromising
> their ecological integrity, diminishing our ability to fully realize
> their potential, costing us jobs and revenue, threatening human
> health, and putting our future at risk.[16]

Overfishing, habitat destruction, invasive species, coastal development, and polluted runoff all threaten to deplete the rich marine

---

16. U.S. Commission on Ocean Policy, "An Ocean Blueprint for the 21st Century,"
   September 20, 2004.

ecosystem, and cause coastal fishermen significant economic hardship. We have an underwater garden of Eden to tend and care for as well, to ensure the ocean continues to teem with life.

Land and Fresh Water

"He set the earth on its foundations; it can never
be moved." (Psalm 104:5)

Vicki and I found ourselves walking uphill through an alley of makeshift booths filled with baskets, tapestries, and ceramic goods made by the indigenous artisans of El Rosario, Michoacan, in the mountains of Central Mexico. We didn't look around. We were not there to shop. We were on a mission to see the *monarcas.*

At about 8,500 feet above sea level, we started noticing occasional monarch butterflies flitting about. The higher we climbed, the more we saw. Soon, we saw them on branches, drinking nectar from flowers, mating, and fluttering everywhere around us. We marveled at the rare sight of such remarkable beauty. "This is nothing; keep going," urged our Mexican guides. Finally, after hiking about forty-five minutes to an elevation of over ten thousand feet, we came face to face with one of the most amazing sights ever witnessed. In the same way that a soft-serve ice-cream cone gets dipped in chocolate, it seemed, someone had taken the pine trees from the mountain forest and dipped them in monarch butterflies! The "topping" was so dense you could no longer see the trunks, branches, or needles of the trees. They were completely covered with multiple layers of living, twinkling gold.

Their story is amazing. Hundreds of millions of butterflies migrate each year to these mountains from all over North America. Some have traveled over two thousand miles, beginning their lives in southeast

Canada. It's impossible to understand how these insects know to come here, let alone how a creature barely an inch and a half long can make the migration, traveling twenty-five to one hundred miles a day.

In their long flight, the swarms of monarchs travel over dense forests, tall prairie, farmland, and the arid southwest. They pass over hundreds of creeks, lakes, and rivers. They see more land than many of us see in a lifetime, but their view is not as pleasant as it used to be.

In Mexico, the forests that provide their winter home are threatened. The very poor mountain people need firewood, and the trees are a convenient source. Up north, the monarch caterpillars live exclusively on native milkweed plants. Rural development and farming practices have greatly reduced the milkweed found in the native prairie. Efforts are underway by volunteers in Mexico, the United States, and Canada to reverse these trends.

When we think about environmental issues, this is the portion of the creation that we most often visualize—the mountains and hills, valleys and plains. We are terrestrial creatures, ground dwellers. Here are the magnificent landscapes that are icons in our minds: the Grand Canyon, Mount Fuji, the Amazon River, the Himalayas, the Sahara Desert, Australia's outback, Yosemite, the Alps, the Everglades, the Arctic tundra. We can't read these names without pictures of the places popping into our mind's eye.

In 1872, the U.S. Congress passed legislation that established the world's first national park at Yellowstone. For the first time, a government said that it was in the best interest of the entire nation to limit the activities allowed on a large tract of land, and the phrase "conservation" entered the American lexicon.

Since then, nearly four hundred other special places have been designated for conservation as national treasures in the United States. Our great-grandparents decided to protect special places by identifying them, defining their boundaries, and adopting special ways to care for them. Their efforts were the beginning of today's "green" movement.

We see the mighty hand of God in these special places, as well as in other places around us. So what is the current state of the plants and animals of our terrestrial world?

Plants

As we raised our daughters, Brooke and Maryn, we spent a fair amount of time hiking in the woods of the Pacific Northwest. I loved to learn about new plants. As you might expect, my girls' eyes would roll as I pointed out differences between dogwoods and cottonwoods, stinging nettles and poison oak, particularly during their teenage years. Yet now they're proud to know more plant names than their friends. How about you—how many plants can you identify? Even the most accomplished botanists have their work cut out for them. Scientists estimate there are about 230,000 to 270,000 species of flowering plants on Earth.

Individual plants are one thing, but the manner in which these plants associate themselves with other plants is yet more evidence of the interconnectedness of creation. Forests are an incredibly important part of the way God created the world. They are home to over three quarters of all the world's plant and animal life. A single acre of forest can absorb enough CO_2 in a year to offset driving a car 26,000 miles. That same acre of forest produces enough oxygen to support eighteen people each day. And remarkably, rain forests also create up to half of their own rainfall by releasing moisture into the air. No wonder forests have been described as the earth's lungs.

Unfortunately, nearly 80 percent of the earth's forests have been removed from the planet. During the past forty years, 20 percent of the

Amazon rain forest has been cut down, and it is projected that an additional 20 percent will be lost in the next twenty years. On the plus side, temperate forests in Europe and America have begun to rebound, increasing by 1 percent in the past fifteen years. However, tropical forests have decreased by about 7 percent in that time. When these large areas of forests disappear, trees convert less CO_2 oxygen and the carbon dioxide therefore remains in the atmosphere, increasing global climate change. As strange as it might seem, it also is common for the areas surrounding removed forests to experience a drought. This effect has been observed in Africa's interior, after rain forests in West Africa have been decimated.

A telling story of cause and effect is at work in the temperate forests in the Pacific Northwest, Western Canada, and Alaska. These forests, usually a lush dark green, are turning red, then brown, and then gray as millions of trees are killed by a natural enemy—the mountain pine beetle. This battle between lodgepole pines and the beetle has raged for millennia, just another balancing act of nature. But recently, the balance has tipped in the beetles' favor.

In the past, several factors limited the range of the mountain pine beetle to the southern Rocky Mountains. One key natural factor—cold winter temperatures—kept the beetles from spreading farther north or to higher altitudes. However, as temperatures have risen in the Northern Hemisphere, the beetles have expanded their range dramatically, thereby affecting additional species of pines at higher elevations, as well as new expanses of forest in Canada and Alaska. Since 1997, beetles have killed 30 million acres of jack and lodgepole pine forests in Canada alone. But that is not the end of the cause and effect story.

While thriving forests absorb carbon dioxide and then release oxygen in its place, dead trees, killed by beetles, are not able to absorb CO_2. As the 30 million acres of dead Canadian trees decompose, they will have precisely the opposite effect—their decay will release 270 million tons of CO_2 into the atmosphere. This, in turn, will speed up global warming, allowing the beetles to spread to new areas and destroy more forest.

Decimated forests are nothing new. The cedars of Lebanon *(Cedrus libani)* were renowned in the ancient world and named repeatedly in the Old Testament. Dense forests of these majestic evergreen trees created habitat for all types of wild animals. King Solomon specified that the temple be constructed from cedars of Lebanon, so that it could be "large and magnificent" (2 Chronicles 2:8–9). Solomon built his own magnificent palace from these trees as well, with four rows of cedar columns supporting forty-five cedar beams. It was so impressive that it was called the "Palace of the Forest of Lebanon" (see 1 Kings 7:2–3). The ancient Jews were not the only ones who treasured this tree. The cedars of Lebanon featured prominently in *The Epic of Gilgamesh,* written about 2000 BC by ancient Sumerians. The epic identified the cedar forests of Lebanon as where the gods dwelled.

As cedars of Lebanon were cut for lumber and other purposes, they were shipped throughout the Near East and cedar became the preferred lumber for many civilizations. The Phoenicians became lumber barons, cutting trees and building ships, which they then used to transport more logs. The Lebanese forests were expansive in ancient times, estimated to cover at least 200,000 acres. However, the Greeks, Romans, Ottoman Empire, and succeeding civilizations each continued to remove trees with little effort toward reforestation. As of today, 98 percent of the historical forest has been removed, and less than 4,200 acres of cedars of Lebanon remain. Of this fractional remnant, the majority is in decline due to impacts from surrounding development. The once mighty forests of Lebanon have been decimated.

In addition to removing plant species, destroying forests has another negative side effect: it removes habitat for animal species.

Animals

There are roughly 44,000 species of animals on the planet—creatures with backbones such as mammals, reptiles, amphibians, birds, and fish. That's 44,000 species out of 1.75 million—the total number of identified species to date. Other than plants and animals, the vast majority of species are insects, crustaceans, and mollusks.

If you're a person of faith, you probably marvel at the incredible animals inhabiting our world. The more I learn about the creatures of this planet, the more awestruck I become. The homing instincts and stamina of our chinook salmon. The maternal behaviors of African elephants. The mating rituals of the sage grouse. The combination of vibrant color and toxic emissions of the poison dart frog. The migratory instincts of songbirds. The endless list of fascinating animals inspired the heroic filmmakers of the 2007 Emmy Award-winning BBC series *Planet Earth.* If you haven't seen the series, do make a point of it. As the beauty of this world demonstrates the creative power of God, the diversity of animals shows us His incredible intelligence and sense of design.

Though the story of Noah may be familiar, it contains a hidden surprise. God was so frustrated with man's pride, hatred, and selfishness that He was sorry He ever brought us into existence. Luckily for us all, God was moved when He found Noah. He decided that this one man carried within him the kernel of hope for the entire human race. With that future in mind, God gave Noah a detailed packing list to ensure that all the wonderful creatures He had created would be preserved to repopulate the earth.

The rain came, the water rose, and humans and animals alike perished. The slate was wiped clean.

> Then God said to Noah and to his sons with him: "I now establish my covenant with you and with your descendants after you and with every living creature that was with you—the birds, the livestock and all the wild animals, all those that came out of the ark with you—every living creature on earth.… Never again will all life be cut off by the waters of a flood." (Genesis 9:8–11)

After the flood, God made a covenant—a binding agreement—with three parties: Noah and his family, his descendants (including us), and *every living creature.* Herein lies the surprise. This was more than a promise not to wipe out people; God's commitment extended to every living creature on the earth. He would never destroy the 44,000 or so species of animals with another great flood. As we discovered in Chapter 3, every one of these was created to praise the Creator. They each are important to him.

Yet unfortunately, humans haven't lived up to the same covenant that God made.

The passenger pigeon, the dodo bird, Caribbean monk seal, golden toad, sea mink, and the Caspian tiger are just a few of the 844 species of animals known to have gone extinct in the past 500 years. And nearly 16,000 plant and animal species are now threatened with extinction, primarily because of the removal of habitat or other human causes.

Each extinction is regretful. But the major regret is that, with every one, we override God's creative genius. There are pragmatic, biological consequences to their loss as well, as animals interact with their habitats in ways that provide services to us, even when we are not aware of them.

Worms and insects cultivate soil, birds consume insects that are harmful to crops, and predators keep rodent populations under control.

"They [smart people who remain passive about environmental destruction] are evidently unaware that ecological services provided scot-free by wild environments, by Eden, are approximately equal in dollar value to the gross world product," notes E.O. Wilson. "They choose to remain innocent of the historical principle that civilizations collapse when their environments are ruined. Most troubling of all, our leaders, including those of the great religions, have done little to protect the living world in the midst of its sharp decline." [17]

In addition to our dependency on natural systems, we are also dependent upon the creatures of creation. Nearly eight hundred years ago, Saint Francis of Assisi made one of the first pro-environment statements outside of the Bible when he said, "These creatures minister to our needs every day; without them we could not live; and through them the human race greatly offends the Creator.... Every day we fail to appreciate so great a blessing."[18]

If God decided the world needed these creatures, shouldn't we who are His followers be leading the way to make sure they survive?

Fresh Water: Lakes, Rivers, and Streams

Clean water. No life can exist without it. We are watery creatures living in a watery world; our bodies are mostly water and over two-thirds of our planet's surface is covered in it. We can go without food for a month, but without water we perish in three to five days.

---

17. E.O. Wilson, *The Creation* (New York: W. W. Norton, 2006), 10.

18. Roger D. Sorrell, *Francis of Assisi and Nature* (New York: Oxford University Press, 1988), 119.

Any threat to our supply of clean water needs to be evaluated seriously. Water shortages may be on our horizon, both here in the United States and worldwide. Global consumption of water is doubling every twenty years. This is more than twice the rate of human population growth.

In 1998, twenty-eight countries in the world had water shortage problems. This number of countries is expected to double by 2025, affecting two-thirds of the world's population. In human terms, about one billion people on the planet do not have access to adequate fresh water, and nearly two and a half billion lack access to adequate sanitation.[19] As the world's population grows and clean water sources decrease due to pollution, this number is likely to increase at a rapid rate. There's hardly need to point out that the scale of human suffering this will create is staggering.

For those of us concerned about the Bible's admonition to care for the "least of these," assuring access to reliable, clean water is an undeniable priority. More than five million people, most of them children, die every year from illnesses caused by drinking poor-quality water. In India, some households have to pay a premium of 25 percent of their income for water. When the World Bank looked at this issue in 1995, vice president Ismail Serageldin came to a sobering conclusion that if the wars of this century were fought over oil, the wars of the next century will be fought over water.

These words have come true much faster than many people anticipated. The seeds of the ethnic civil war in the Darfur region of Sudan were sown in the devastating drought that occurred in the late 1980s. In 2003, the drought and lack of access to water for farming caused an

---

19. World Health Organization, "Almost Half the World's People Have No Acceptable Means of Sanitation," Press Release WHO/73, November 22, 2000, www.who.int/inf-pr-2000/en/pr2000-73.html.

uprising of citizens against the government. In this horrendous civil conflict, it is estimated that over 300,000 people have died since 2003.

Standing in defiance of the growing scarcity of fresh water are those of us who live in the United States. The United Nations reports that people need a minimum of thirteen gallons a day for drinking, washing, cooking, and sanitation. Here in the United States, each of us uses about 100 to 150 gallons a day. This daily amount varies with the amount we use outdoors for gardening, sprinklers, swimming pools, and other outdoor uses. By comparison, each person in Morocco uses twenty-nine gallons per day, about one-fifth as much as we use. But that's just Morocco, right? In Great Britain, the average Brit uses thirty-one gallons per day, and the average German, forty-one gallons per day. If there is a water shortage that hurts "the least of these," it looks like we have some work to do in conserving water.[20]

• • •

This is the current state of our planet. The air, ocean, land, and fresh water resources given to us by the Creator are suffering. The garden is in decline. There are pragmatic reasons to be concerned, economic reasons to alter our course, and spiritual reasons to consider a new way of living.

But within the community of faith, where is the concern, the sense of urgency? Until gasoline hit four dollars a gallon, people did not seem too concerned about conserving oil or reducing emissions or about the health of the environment in general. So what keeps people from becoming more involved in conservation? What are our biggest objections?

---

20. Pacific Institute, "The World's Water, Table 2: Freshwater Withdrawal by Country and Sector (2006 update)," www.worldwater.org/data.html.

6

The Big Push-Back

All of us live under the same sky,
but we don't all have the same horizon.

—Konrad Adenauer

Mike, do you think it's valid for Christians to hold one of myriad opposing viewpoints on global warming and act on the environment accordingly?"

So began the first of five questions e-mailed to me after speaking to a church in Portland on Earth Day, 2007. My response began, "No. I am right, and everyone should be like me (insert emoticon here)."

Pulling my tongue out of my cheek, I went on to say that of course I believe that disagreement on many of the issues of the day is to be expected, even among people of a similar faith. However, in spite of our differences, Psalm 133:1 and Colossians 3:13–14 tell us that if we are people of faith, we should live in unity with one another. As long as we agree on the critical tenets of the faith, we are bound together as brothers and sisters. Incumbent in that is for me to listen to the beliefs of others about issues (such as their views about environmental stewardship and other topics), consider their rationale, and share with them my rationale as well. I believe that as we study God's Word and learn new things, we are encouraged to share what we learn with others. But if God doesn't give others the same understanding I've received, then we continue to dwell together, unified by our love and appreciation of our diverse lives.

I have long noticed a lack of interest in environmental issues on the part of people who consider themselves Jews or Christians. People who normally are quite opinionated on issues of morality often seem indifferent to smog, climate change, urban sprawl and congestion, oil spills, or the extinction of plant and animal species. Though my friends love the beauty of creation and diligently strive to fulfill God's will in other areas of their lives, they seem remarkably indifferent to environmental issues. Why would people who consider themselves purposely faithful seem apathetic about caring for creation?

Why, indeed. In my conversations with people of all stripes, political leanings, and economic and educational levels, several common objections have emerged. Some objections seem to spring from a theological base, while others seem to be political gut reactions. I realized that for my own benefit, I couldn't leave these objections unevaluated. Soon, I found myself writing down the objections and considering them in detail. I read books, consulted experts, and discussed the issues with theologians. And I spent a great deal of time in the Scriptures. In this process, some of my ideas changed while others became more certain. For me, the issue moved from a cognitive issue to a spiritual one. I was also humbled. Rather than congratulating myself about my green perspective, God showed me that I, too, had a long way to go to be the responsible steward He wants me to be.

Following are some of the most common objections to creation care I have heard and my thoughts about each.

1. "God gave us the earth to use, so don't sweat it."

We discussed this objection earlier, but this line of reasoning basically lays out like this: Since God created the world and then man and told the first man to be fruitful and multiply, this planet is just like a giant bank account of natural resources that God gave us access to. We didn't deposit the equity in the account; God did. But it is here for our use and enjoyment. Therefore, we don't really need to worry about protecting it.

This description sounds more like a trust-fund scenario than a limited checking account—a limitless pool of riches that can be drawn from on a whim, with little or no concern for the future. Creation, according to this view, is a no-strings gift for humankind; we can do whatever we want with it.

A number of years back, the U.S. government sent me to assist in the planning of a new national park in the Central African Republic. In the southwest corner of the country, wedged between Cameroon and the Congo is one of the last remaining intact sections of tropical rain forest in Africa. Home to gorillas, chimpanzees, forest elephants, and Baka pygmy people, this is a magical place. It is one of the most remote places on earth.

There was a great deal of pressure to log the area, to extract the timber resources of the rain forest. Paradoxically, most of the income from logging would have gone to a Belgian timber company, not the locals. The U.S. government sent me at the request of the Central African Republic government and the World Wildlife Fund. My assignment: to see if it would be possible to develop an alternative economic model for the area.

A colleague and I spent over a month in the jungle evaluating the feasibility of replacing an economy dependent upon the extraction of these incredible resources with an economy based on protecting them: ecotourism. Ecological tourism appeals to people who are socially minded, environmentally interested, and willing to trade creature comforts for adventure. The Dzanga-Sangha region certainly qualifies: few comforts and many opportunities for adventure.

One day my companion and I had to head down the Sangha River in a small dugout canoe powered by a tiny outboard motor. The river was wide and brown, with no discernable current. We floated through warm chocolate pudding, which barely qualified as liquid. The electric pulses of insects in the overhanging trees buzzed in our ears as we passed. The air was hot and thick with humidity. Even at a nominal speed, moving downriver brought cooling air across my sweaty neck. The skipper and first mate of my hollowed-out-log canoe were two armed rangers. Employees of the government, their job was to stop poachers from killing chimps, gorillas, and any other forest animals.

Suddenly, one of the rangers shouted sharply and pointed downriver. The other replied, and they gunned the little outboard engine until it sounded like a chorus of cicadas. Looking into the sun, my colleague and I could not see what it was that had attracted their attention. Was it a poacher? Were we headed for an armed battle?

As I squinted through my sunglasses, I did notice a small piece of wood or debris floating on the river surface. Could this be what the rangers were excited about? As we continued to gain on this floating debris, it became increasingly apparent that this was their target. As we approached, I saw that it was not a log after all. It was some type of animal, swimming in the current. Though I could see it was alive, I could not identify what type of animal it was—reptile, mammal, or bird.

As we drew alongside, one of the rangers reached over the side, grabbed the animal by the tail, and hoisted it in the air. Over four feet long, with four legs, a long tail, and a long snout, the creature looked like a cross between an armadillo and an anteater. I asked the rangers in broken French

"Qu'est-ce qui est cela?" (What is that?)

"Pangolin," they replied.

The giant pangolin is a remarkable animal. Although it looks like some mutated crocodile or other reptile, it is actually a mammal. When threatened, pangolins pull a trick they must have learned from the lowly sow bug: they roll up into a ball, leaving nothing but their armored plates exposed. Sometimes called scaly anteaters, pangolins live in the equatorial portions of the African continent, from West Africa to Uganda.

But pangolins are in trouble. They live on the ants and termites found in tropical rain forests. As these rain forests are cut down, so goes their food supply. In addition, they are hunted aggressively as a type of "bush meat," a fate that faces all the animals in the jungle.

Well, this big guy is thankfully in good hands, I thought. *The rangers have rescued it from drowning in the river and will carry it to shore.* The ranger placed it in the bottom of the canoe, where it immediately made itself into a scaly cannonball for protection.

95

A few minutes later, the pangolin began to unroll in the bottom of the canoe. In an instant, the ranger held the pangolin's head down with his foot and delivered a fatal blow with his machete.

"Why did you kill it?" I asked the rangers. "I thought you were supposed to be protecting the animals in the area?"

"Yes, but pangolin is very delicious, and my wife will be very pleased."

It is not only those of us living in highly technological cultures who have problems restraining ourselves.

Our instinct (human nature) tells us to get what we can, right now. Our faith teaches us that we should sacrifice for others and trust God for the future. Wisdom requires us to view the created world and all its resources as gifts, treasures that we want to ensure are available for our great-great-grandchildren's great-great-grandchildren. If we discipline ourselves in the ways we utilize the resources of the planet, we will be seen as wise and effective caretakers by future generations, as well as by the Creator. If we don't, we will leave a damaged garden to the generations that come after and will be held accountable.

For most of human history, the natural world has often been a hostile, threatening place. Nomadic herdsman built protective barriers to protect their flocks at night from predators. As hunter-gatherers gradually learned to be farmers, they cleared dense forests, with their incredible diversity of plant and animal species, in order to support agriculture. As people began to settle in cities and industrial development ensued, we became less and less directly dependent upon natural forces.

In fact, our expanding technology has allowed us to thwart nature and natural processes. We built jetties to stop waves, erected dams to halt rivers, paved ground to keep it from absorbing rain, and developed climate-controlled interior environments that allow us to go days without ever coming in contact with the "real" weather.

As we disconnected ourselves from the processes of the natural world, our philosophies and cultures changed as well. No longer were we dependent upon each other, held together in communities for our common good. The individual assumed preeminence, and the natural world became a limitless pantry. As author and philosophy professor Roger S. Gottlieb observes in his book *A Greener Faith*,

> For the most part, the industrialized world views nature as a resource to be exploited: a mass of animals and plants, minerals and water, whose purpose is to serve humanity. This fundamentally human-centered…perspective on nature, many theologians believe, is at the core of the crisis. It justifies thoughtless devastation of anything that gets in our way or looks like it might come in handy.[1]

---

1. Roger S. Gottlieb, *A Greener Faith* (New York: Oxford University Press, 2006), 21–22.

But is this what God had in mind when He gave us responsibility for gardening Eden? Did He intend that we should take whatever we want rather than what we need? Did He give people unlimited sovereignty with no strings attached, or was it His intent that we demonstrate responsibility with accountability? Is it acceptable if our desires supersede the needs of the rest of creation? Are people more important? And which people are we talking about—those alive today or those yet to come?

As mentioned earlier, this sounds very different from the principles of stewardship that God reveals in the Old and New Testaments.

However, there is a grain of truth here. God did create this planet to support humans and all other living things. He did give us the right to use the resources here to meet our needs. However, the "us" is all of humankind—past, present, and future—with each individual generation receiving from its predecessors the responsibility to care for and steward this planet on behalf of untold succeeding generations. What my generation does with creation may greatly affect what future generations are left to steward. We can't disrupt nature without impacting people. As C.S. Lewis said, "What we call Man's power over Nature turns out to be a power exercised by some men over other men with Nature as its instrument."[2]

We are a "needy" people; but the concept of "needs" has mushroomed in our day and age. At the dawn of a new millennium, we find ourselves falling into the trap of desiring instant gratification in many areas of our lives, from our eating habits to our finances to our relationships. When we are honest, we admit that we often have trouble differentiating between wants and needs. We have even created magazines such as *Real Simple* that feature the ironic benefits of purchasing new items that will simplify your life.

97

2. C.S. Lewis, *The Abolition of Man* (New York: HarperCollins Publishers, 1944), 55.

We have grown accustomed to mortgaging the future for the pleasures of today. Our culture's entire economy seems to be built on this tenet. I'd say many of us are addicted to a lifestyle predicated upon:

ME

MORE

NOW

In our hearts, we know that this is wrong. We acknowledge that, although God gave us the vast resources of this planet to meet our needs, He expects us to practice restraint and willingly make sacrifices that will provide benefits for others, today and in the future.

2. "It doesn't really matter—the planet is going to be destroyed anyway."

People ask, "Isn't the planet going to burn anyway? Don't 2 Peter 3 and Hebrews 1 say that this world will come to an end? If it's all ultimately going to be destroyed, what does it matter if it's not in pristine condition when it goes?"

Yes, like our physical bodies, this earth will be transformed in ways we do not yet understand. However, the earth will not be annihilated or wiped from the universe. God is not admitting defeat or failure and asking for a "do over." Instead, the earth will be transformed into the creation that God originally intended, not marred by sadness, violence, or pain.

Jesus explained the coming New Age as a *renewal* of all things, not a destruction and re-creation (see Matthew 19:28). Something renewed is recognizable as the original, but fresh, clean, pure, and "in like-new condition." The risen Christ returned to this same theme in Revelation 21 when he said that he was making everything on heaven and earth new.

In the first days of the neophyte Christian church, the apostle Peter preached that Jesus "must remain in heaven until the time comes for God to restore everything, as he promised long ago through his holy prophets" (Acts 3:21).

Note that Jesus is coming to *restore* everything, not remake it or re-create it. As Randy Alcorn states in his book *Heaven,*

> We're told that a time is coming when God will restore *every-thing*. This is an inclusive promise. It encompasses far more than God merely restoring disembodied people to fellowship in a spirit realm.... It is God restoring mankind to what we once were, what he designed us to be—fully embodied, right-eous beings. And restoring the entire physical universe to what it once was....
>
> God will restore everything *on Earth*. The prophets are never concerned about some far-off realm of disembodied spirits. They are concerned about the land, the inheritance, the city of Jerusalem, and the earth they walked on. Messiah will come from Heaven to Earth, not to take us away from Earth to Heaven, but to restore Earth to what he intended so he can live with us here forever.
>
> Will the earth we know come to an end? Yes. To a *final* end? No.[3]

Perhaps people have found it convenient to think that this earth is going to be eliminated. Such thinking takes away the pressure to practice sacrificial stewardship. Maybe a faulty understanding of eternity has

---

3. Randy Alcorn, *Heaven* (Wheaton, IL: Tyndale House, 2004), 90.

allowed us to abrogate our responsibility. But just because the earth will be transformed doesn't give us the right to disregard or even trash it now. As appealing as it is, I'm sure this do-over vision of the future is not God's plan.

It's interesting that we don't use that same line of reasoning in talking about other areas of our lives: "Since I know I'm going to die anyway, I don't need to worry about my health," "I don't really need to think of my body as the temple of God," or "Well, you know, after I die and go to heaven, there won't be any finances, so it doesn't really matter if I live financially irresponsibly here on earth." Instead, we at least recognize that we should be effective stewards of our resources, our health, and our time.

Since Scripture tells us that the earth is going to be renewed rather than eliminated and replaced, we should consider the potential eternal consequences of our activities here and now, both for our spiritual health and for the earth's physical health. In the same way that Jesus's wounds were visible to His disciples after His resurrection, perhaps the scars we cause on the planet will be visible for all eternity, even in a renewed earth. Maybe the great strip mines of Montana, the damming of the Three Rivers Gorge in China, and the sterile wasteland that was once dense tropical rain forests will persist into eternity. But even if not, we will have to explain ourselves and the way we treated His creation.

Jesus talked quite a bit about accountability. In the parables of the faithful servant, the ten bridesmaids, and the talents recorded in Matthew 24 and 25, He took pains to emphasize the importance of doing the right thing all the time and not counting on being bailed out by some remarkable event. The parables tell us to fulfill our responsibilities, use our resources carefully, and invest wisely for the future.

From these and many other biblical parables, I learn that I should be grateful for this planet and nurture it always—the Master or the Bridegroom could return at any time and catch me in the act. And He's not real fond of excuses.

3. "People are more important than nature."

Since God has made people more important than the rest of creation and has actually given us dominion over creation, it doesn't matter what happens to creation. We are the priority, not the created world around us. (Ah, it is so easy to place ourselves at the center of the universe. In fact, in this argument, we come dangerously close to placing ourselves, not God, on the throne.)

Asking which is more important to God—people or nature—is a loaded question. People are much closer to God's heart than the rest of creation, aren't we?

Of course. People are God's crowning creation. He created us in His own image, for heaven's sake! He willingly sacrificed His own Son to bring us back into proper relationship with Him. So people are, in fact, special to Him. And yet, as we have seen, the creation is important to God. It's not quite as if God votes "man" instead of "creation." He made both, loves both, and expects man to demonstrate that he can live in such a way that both are nurtured here on earth.

God reserves a special place for the people He placed on this earth, but with this honor He expects humility. Our elevated status comes with something not expected of creation at large—responsibility. Once again, this expectation is similar to what God expects of parents who have been given "dominion" over their children.

We are held accountable by how we fulfill our responsibilities; if we are poor stewards of creation, God will not be pleased.

Man does have a special status in God's eyes; after all we are created "in his own image" (Genesis 1:27). However, God was pleased that through Christ, all things in creation—not just man—could be reconciled to Him (see Colossians 1:19-20). It is clear that woven throughout Scripture is an additional message: man is an important part of God's creation, but not the only important part. God loves it all: mountains, seas, plants, animals, and man. And His desire is that we all thrive. Together.

We are not the owner of creation—God is. We are as dependent upon creation as are our fellow creatures. We share another similarity: both the creation and the creature man are unhappy with our current state, a frustration so intense it causes creation and man alike to groan in severe pain. We share a desperate longing to be freed from the degrading effects of sin on our planet and within our souls.

The creation is not what it was intended to be, and neither are we. But in the same way that God doesn't approve of us mistreating other fallen humans, He does not give us authority to degrade the environment either. In a manner very similar to the way our physical bodies will be transformed at Christ's return, the creation will also be "liberated from its bondage to decay" (Romans 8:21). This is our source of hope.

People are not the only part of creation that is dear to God. We must respect the importance of the natural world, as God does.

4. "Environmental protection hurts the economy."

"SAVE A LOGGER, EAT A SPOTTED OWL!"

Sometimes a bumper sticker can aptly summarize a complex social struggle. Here in the Pacific Northwest, the wounds are still raw from the battle between those fighting to protect the last few acres of primitive forest and those fighting to protect the last few logging jobs. Although publicized as "jobs versus owls," this was never really the case. The fight centered on whether or not to protect the roughly 5 percent of remaining unlogged forest in the Cascade Range of the West Coast, which met the unique habitat needs of the northern spotted owl and many other plants and animals. Scientists believed that this type of forest was unique and had been almost completely eradicated from the planet. New labels were invented to describe this type of undisturbed, wet, mountainous habitat with giant trees: it was called ancient, old-growth, primeval, or virgin forest.

In the 1990s, it came down to this simple decision: was it in the public's best interest to preserve these remaining stands of forest, or was it better to allow them to be logged to provide raw wood material and jobs?

The spotted owl became the poster child in the environment vs. economy debate.

Of course, had it been a century or two earlier, the debate would not have been so heated. Then, with millions of acres of forest covering the land and our limited technological ability to impact it, no one imagined that protection was necessary. However, by the late twentieth century, the tiny remnant of remaining forest had everyone up in arms. Environmentalists successfully argued in the federal courts that these stands of forests were such a unique resource that the long-term health of the environment required their protection.

Both sides were guilty of hyperbole and exaggeration. Timber jobs had already been declining for two decades before the spotted owl flap. Increased automation, not endangered species, was to blame for the loss of jobs. The industry needed fewer and fewer loggers to cut, move, and process the logs. A 1999 study by the University of Wisconsin found that "the 1989 [Endangered Species] listing of the spotted owl has no significant effect on employment—not even in the two states where the debate has been most intense," Oregon and Washington.[4]

On the other side, the spotted owl and its reclusive habits made generating accurate population estimates difficult. And habitat loss turned out not to be the only significant threat to the spotted owl. Competition from the barred owl, another species that has moved into the Pacific Northwest from the East Coast, has proven as threatening to the northern spotted owl as logging. Barred owls are more aggressive than their cousins, and they likely harass, displace, and mate with spotted owls. So, in either case, the future of the spotted owl is far from settled.

But the Northwest Forest Plan, enacted by Congress in 1994, sought to preserve the remaining forest for all species, including humans and owls. It did so by attempting to achieve a balance between producing a predictable and sustainable amount of timber products and protecting the long-term health of the forests.

The Forest Plan was an experiment to see if it was possible to protect the environment while ensuring that the economy remained strong. Interestingly enough (and not just due to the Forest Plan) the economy in the Pacific Northwest accelerated in the 1990s. The Pacific Northwest led the nation in growth with the lowest unemployment levels in the country.

So, do we have to choose between environmental protection and economic performance?

After conducting an extensive review of economic studies designed

---

4. William Freudenburg and Lisa J. Wilson, "Forty Years of Spotted Owls? A Longitudinal Analysis of Logging Industry Job Losses," University of Wisconsin-Madison, published in *Sociological Perspectives,* Pacific Sociological Association 41, no. 1 (1998), 1–26.

to evaluate the connection between environmental protection and economic degradation, John R. E. Bliese, author of *The Greening of Conservative America,* notes these findings:

- Total spending on environment protection is approximately 2 percent of the U.S. gross domestic product. "There is no evidence that the economy has been adversely affected as a whole by strong environmental protection policies."[5]

- Within industries, companies that pollute at low levels are no less profitable than those that pollute at much higher levels. "There is simply no evidence that superior environmental performance puts firms at a market disadvantage or adversely affects market performance"[6]

- Those U.S. states that have the highest levels of environmental protection also exhibit the highest levels of economic performance.[7]

- A study by the Harvard Business School identified numerous cases where new environmental regulations led to advances in technology, processes, or products, resulting in companies becoming more competitive and profitable.[8]

In 1997, more than 2,500 prominent U.S. economists, including nine Nobel Laureates, came to similar conclusions and signed a comprehensive statement that looked at global climate change as a tremendous economic opportunity for the country. In a profession where consensus

---

5. "Report on U.S. Environmental Performance," Organization for Economic Cooperation and Development, (February 1996).

6. Robert Repetto, "Jobs, Competitiveness and Environmental Regulation: What are the Real Issues?" World Resources Institute (1995).

7. Roger Bezdek, "Environment and Economy: What's the Bottom Line?" Environment 35 (September 1993).

8. Michael Portert and Claas van der Linde, "Green and Competitive," Harvard Business Review (September/October 1995).

is difficult, if not impossible, the fact that these experts reached an agreement is remarkable. Among other things, their statement said:

> Economic studies have found that there are many potential policies to reduce greenhouse-gas emissions for which the total benefits outweigh the total costs. For the United States…there are policy options that would slow climate change without harming American living standards, and these measures may in fact improve U.S. productivity in the long run.[9]

Bliese sums up this way: "There have been dozens of well-designed studies by economists who have tested these claims, and the results are clear: environmental protection normally has no negative impact on the economy overall, and sometimes it has a positive effect."[10]

Private businesses have responded. Many have recognized that being more efficient with resources will have a positive effect on the bottom line. "Eco-efficiency" has become an important objective for many companies, and has helped to combine environmental and economic business issues. In June 2000, the World Business Council for Sustainable Development, in partnership with many international corporations, developed a new accounting methodology. Pilot companies that participated in this program included 3M, Proctor & Gamble, Toyota, and General Motors.[11]

---

9. "The Economists' Statement on Climate Change," March 29, 1997, www.rprogress.org/publications/1997/econstatement.htm.

10. John R. E. Bliese, "The Great 'Environment Versus Economy' Myth," *The Green Elephant* (Summer 1999).

11. "Measuring Eco-Efficiency: A Guide to Reporting Company Performance," by Hendrik Verfallie of Monsanto Company and Robin Bidwell of Environmental Resources Management LLC, World Business Council for Sustainable Development (June 2000).

As we look around us, these market realities are alive and well today. Sales of Toyota's hybrid Prius have eclipsed the sales of Ford's Explorer. The renewable energy sector is robust, with wind and solar power becoming significant sources of research and development capital. When consumer demand changes, supply changes to meet it. New jobs that are based on conservation are replacing others that relied on resource extraction. In the long run, environmental protection will not hurt the economy. In fact, an entire new industry is emerging that holds great potential for providing significant high-wage jobs.

5. "Environmental protection is just another abuse of power by big government."

In my career, I have spent about sixteen years in the private sector, most of that as a small business owner, and another thirteen years in the public sector. I am currently the planning director for the city of Gresham, Oregon, population 100,000. So it is fair to say that I have seen both sides of the debate.

After a recent talk I gave on creation care, I got an e-mail from someone in the audience. He told me about a relative living in a European country with a number of "extremist environmental" laws. For example, the relative is required to keep a certain percentage of his property "green." Because the house is large and the lot small, a portion of the roof had to be "covered by moss." "Would I support such a socialist requirement here in the United States?" he asked.

This forced mossing sounds a bit ridiculous at first blush, doesn't it? However, it may not be. Though I am not privy to the specifics of the situation, here is one plausible explanation.

When rain falls from the sky and hits a roof, paved street, or other impermeable surface, it runs off the surface. Usually to the street, then along a gutter, into a catch basin, and from there into an underground sewer pipe. If the property is in a city like Portland, which has an old sewer system where storm runoff is combined with good ol' sewage, the pipe runs underground until it reaches a sewage treatment plant. Everything that happens from the edge of the private property line is paid for by taxpayers like you and me. That means we pay for and own all the sewer pipes, manholes, and pumps, as well as the sewer treatment plant itself. The more runoff in the sewer system, the larger the pipes and the treatment plant need to be. These plants are often $100 million to $1 billion expenditures; not exactly chump change! Who pays for all this infrastructure? Local citizens like you and me. The less runoff and sewage in the system, the smaller this infrastructure can be, and the less we have to pay.

So, in cities like Portland, there is an effort to get people to reduce the amount of rainwater that ends up in the sewer system. Here's where the moss could fit in. You may have heard the term "green roof" or "eco-roof." This is where a roof contains a small amount of soil in which plants are grown. These green roofs are terrific reservoirs for rainwater, dramatically slowing down and reducing the amount that runs off into the underground sewer system. By trapping rainwater on the site, they keep it from driving up the size of the public infrastructure. These roofs have existed in older European cities for hundreds of years and have proven to be very watertight with a much longer life than conventional roofs.

This is why many cities and utility districts are beginning to offer incentives such as lower sewer fees to property owners who disconnect their downspouts from the city's sewer system. If we can keep as much water on individual properties rather than in the sewer system, it is less likely that we will need to build bigger, more centralized, and more expensive treatment infrastructure. Decentralized systems are smaller and less expensive. Perhaps moss on a roof ends up benefiting everyone in the long run.

So something that initially sounds ridiculous may make sense once we delve a bit deeper, if we are willing to go beyond a knee-jerk reaction against "big government."

What is the purpose of government, anyway? None other than Alexander Hamilton, the conservative founding father, asked this question in Federalist Papers #15:

"Why has government been instituted at all?"

This free trade advocate and first Secretary of the Treasury went on to answer his own question:

"Because the passions of men will not conform to the dictates of reason and justice, without constraint."

Even Hamilton recognized the tension between the economic forces that drive progress and the overall public good. We appreciate the power of economic interests to improve our lives, but we recognize the need for restraints. We don't want a polluting factory built in our neighborhood, even though it may be highly profitable. We are outraged when companies lie about the health risks of their products while watching profits soar. In his compelling book *Hurtling Toward Oblivion,* futurist and author Richard Swenson puts it this way:

> In sheer power and influence, economics now dwarfs all other forces in modern society....
>
> Because progress and the economy are directly related, progress is not going to slow down. We can count on *more and more of everything faster and faster* from here on out because the economy requires it.[12]

---

12. Richard A. Swenson, *Hurtling Toward Oblivion,* (Colorado Springs: NavPress, 1999), 44.

109

Hamilton and the other founding fathers understood the incredible power of capitalism. They knew that providing incentive for success needed to be a key building block of our nation. Capitalism rewards entrepreneurship.

However, the founding fathers also recognized that the democracy needed constraining pressures as well. Living without limits is not healthy. Therefore, our democracy places constraints upon all of us to ensure that the overall public good is not sacrificed while a few profit. We may disagree with how big government should be, but we all see the need for the checks and balances government provides.

As a consultant, I worked with a broad variety of private corporations with various agendas. Many of my clients were development companies motivated primarily by short-term profits. They often did not want to hear about limits. I was told to do as little as possible—but nothing more—to have a project approved by government officials. I was grateful when a city or other jurisdiction had regulations that prevented my client from doing ecological and social harm, such as polluting streams, filling sensitive wetlands, or creating ugly, unsafe neighborhoods. I also realized that these regulations don't just appear at the whim of a bureaucrat. They are almost always initiated by concerned citizens who see a need to establish limits.

This is a novel concept for our times—establishing limits, on ourselves or on corporations.

In our market-based economy, should we expect a company to establish limits on its own profits? In 2007, when gasoline cost more than three dollars per gallon, ExxonMobil reported the highest profits ever for a U.S. company—$40.6 billion. That's a profit of nearly $1,300 per second! Yet the day that these record profits were announced, the value of Exxon shares actually *declined* on the stock market. Apparently, ExxonMobil's record profits were not quite high enough for investors.

Business is not designed to place limits on itself. Regardless of how many or how few constraints are placed upon them, businesses will continue to do what they do—try to maximize profits. They do this with little concern about the welfare of future generations. Of course it's not faceless businesses that make these decisions. It's people like you and me—people who, like most of us, tend to choose short-term gain over long-term stewardship.

However, the longer-term perspective has to come from citizens like you and me. We elect government officials to represent us. We buy products and services from corporations, and we may even become shareholders. In other words, you and I are the ones who establish the limits on business. We are the ones who decide whether or not oil companies can drill in the Arctic National Wildlife Refuge. We are the ones who determine if we are willing to make changes in our lifestyles to decrease global warming. We are the ones who decide if public funds should be spent to build mass transit and parks or purchase lands for preservation. We decide which businesses we will patronize by our shopping habits. This is not a question of us versus the government. Rather, in a paraphrase of the famous quote by the cartoon character Pogo: "We have met the government, and he is us."

Environmental protection is not a result of big government. Rather it is an outcome of private citizens like you and me deciding that protecting creation is important, both personally and nationally.

● ● ●

The five objections to environmental stewardship that I've considered here are certainly not the only objections people raise. Yet they each make us face our own basic character flaws—pride, greed, and a tendency toward a limited, earthly, short-term perspective.

The great news is, environmental stewardship was designed to be a joy, and this remains God's intent in the twenty-first century. We feel no fulfillment if our motives are built upon guilt or legalism. Rather, our commitment to environmental stewardship must come forth naturally from our great love and appreciation of the Creator. In fact, this is the source of true worship.

7

Creation Care as Worship

God writes the Gospel, not in the Bible alone,
but also on trees, and flowers, and clouds, and stars.

—MARTIN LUTHER

The happiest man is he who learns
from nature the lesson of worship.

—RALPH WALDO EMERSON

When we truly pause to consider it, creation is overwhelming. It is big and brash, dwarfing us and making our lives seem inconsequential by comparison. It is beauty in the face of incredible ruggedness. Order in spite of inestimable complexity. Unity in spite of infinite detail. Reflect on all of this, and it is understandable if you drop to your knees. To paraphrase a common bumper sticker, "If you aren't awestruck, you're not paying attention."

The creation should drive us to our knees. Not to worship *it*, but to worship the One who made it happen. His genius, His power, His wisdom. All of which combined to cause creation's beauty, creation's diversity, creation's order. But really seeing the creation takes awareness on our part; we have to pay attention.

If we are to walk creation's path to worship, we will have to involve all parts of ourselves: our senses, our minds, our spirits, and our hands.

Opening Our Eyes: The Step of Observation

The first step along creation's path to worship is observation—opening our eyes to see the real beauty that exists in the world around us. Yet, our observation skills have grown weak, often rendering us oblivious to the beauty which surrounds. Most of us are so task-oriented and driven by the tyranny of the urgent that we fail to stop and smell (or even see) the roses. With our attention diverted by the cares of life, we miss being inspired by the glorious sunset, the quaking leaves of fall, or Beethoven's "Ode to Joy." When we fail to be astute observers of all creation, we miss the things that can truly feed our souls.

In the early 1800s, a new landscape painter captured the imagination of the American public. His name was Thomas Cole, and he painted in the Adirondack, Catskill, and White Mountains of upstate New York and New England. One of the founders of the Hudson River School of Art, Cole influenced many other artists with his romantic and allegorical depictions of nature. Cole, who was a keen observer of scenery, felt it was important to recognize that nature's beauty was "the visible hand of God." As Cole wrote:

> He who looks on nature with a "loving eye," cannot move from
> his dwelling without the salutation of beauty; even in the city
> the deep blue sky and the drifting clouds appeal to him.... The
> delight such a man experiences is not merely sensual, or selfish,
> that passes with the occasion leaving no trace behind; but in
> gazing on the pure creations of the Almighty, he feels a calm
> religious tone steal through his mind, and when he has turned
> to mingle with his fellow men, the chords which have been
> struck in that sweet communion cease not to vibrate.[1]

We're not merely talking about "eye candy" here. There is something deep within each of us that stirs when we contemplate a beauti-

---

1. Thomas Cole, "Essay on American Scenery," *American Monthly Magazine* (January 1836).

ful scene. If we allow it to run its natural course, this stirring can lead us to worship—worship not of the scene, but of the One behind the scene.

This can work one of two ways. First, experiencing beauty can take us by surprise, leading us unexpectedly to stop, take a breath, and express our worship to the Creator. However, it can also be much more intentional. If you are looking to cultivate an attitude of worship, find a way to insert beauty into your life. A natural scene, a work of art, or great music works for me. We can start the worship process by opening our eyes and seeing the beauty around us.

For me, yesterday was a bird day. I am not much of a birder, but as time goes by and I see new types of birds in my backyard, I'm becoming more interested. Normally, we have house finches and chickadees on the bird feeder, with red-shafted flickers and downy woodpeckers on the suet log, and mallard ducks in the creek. The flickers are my favorite. They are big birds—a foot long—looking almost hand painted in their intricacy of pattern and color.

But yesterday was a remarkable day. The songbirds must have stopped in Fairview as they migrated north for the summer. In addition to the bright reds of the male house finches, I was surprised to see the electric yellow of American goldfinches on the feeder. Diving for bugs along the creek was a flock of yellow-rumped warblers. Western scrub-jays, robins, thrushes, and bushtits also filled the air.

Looking out the window of my study, I saw the aerial acrobatics of dozens of swallows as they swept the air clean of hatching insects. I have long wondered what type of swallows they were—they move so fast that they are nearly impossible to see clearly through binoculars. I figured they had to be either tree swallows or violet-green swallows, but I couldn't see them clearly from inside the house. For some reason, yesterday I was moved to step outside.

I walked out to the front of the house and headed the fifty feet or so to where our street crosses Fairview Creek. As I stood on the bridge, the darting, swooping swallows surrounded me. There were so many of them, and they were so close, that images of South Pacific vacationers surrounded by dolphins came to mind. I was swimming with the swallows! Suddenly, I didn't need any binoculars to see them clearly; they were right in front of my face, albeit for an instant. Immediately, it became obvious that they were violet-green swallows, iridescent with their metallic green backs and purple tails and all snowy white underneath. They seemed to be performing just for my benefit. As I stood transfixed by their acrobatics and beauty, I was moved to worship and thank God for allowing me to experience this display of His creation. I felt strangely honored by the experience.

So, here was the lesson for me: for over two years I had seen these active birds and wondered what they were. But until yesterday, I never got out of my chair to experience them. I moved from being a passive wonderer to a sincere experiencer of this small aspect of creation. And I received a rich reward—an experience not to be forgotten.

Transforming Our Minds: The Step of Solitude

Another step on creation's path to worship is experiencing the power of solitude. It goes hand in hand with observation. Being able to see the beauty in the world around us requires that we open our eyes, but observation is even more powerful if we are alone with our thoughts.

This is the pattern modeled by Christ Himself. He prepared for three intense years of ministry by withdrawing to the desert for forty days of solitude, where He contemplated stones, mountains, and His spiritual adversary. His ministry was marked by an ebb and flow of contact with others. He would draw away to a "lonely place" for a time to commune with His Father and then return to the crowds who wanted so much from Him.

We, too, find ourselves inundated with the pressures of life and the expectations of others. Like Christ, we are in need of recharging our spiritual batteries. Creation's garden can be a wonderful stage upon which to practice solitude.

Solitude can enhance our appreciation of the environment. Time spent alone can be a powerful way to remove the distractions that commonly prevent us from approaching God in a fully yielding, open way. Spending time alone in creation allows our minds to reflect on the majesty of creation and the omnipotence of the Creator. Our minds can be re-created, refreshed, and recharged. Richard Foster calls this "the re-creating stillness of solitude."[2]

When I think of being re-created, I can't help being reminded of Nicodemus's confusion when he asked Jesus, "How can a man be born again?" Likewise I ask: how can we be re-created?

Perhaps we find the answer in Jesus's reply to Nicodemus: "So it is with everyone born of the Spirit." Re-creation is a spiritual process, one that replaces distractions with stillness and focuses our attention on our spiritual relationship with the Creator. Solitude sets the stage for re-creation, but the Spirit does the work in us.

Does that mean that we must strap on a backpack and head for the high country? That could work, but so might taking an hour to sit on a bench in a nearby park, perching on a rock alongside a nearby stream, or heading for the beach. Parking your car for a few minutes to watch

2. Richard Foster, *Celebration of Discipline: The Path to Spiritual Growth,* (New York: HarperCollins, 1998), 97–98.

the sun set can provide powerful moments of connection with the Creator. A bike ride along a winding pathway can provide precious moments to reflect on God's goodness.

Replacing noise with stillness is a challenge in today's culture. The distractions of sight and sound are ubiquitous. Where can we escape blaring televisions, chiming computers, beeping PDAs, and attention-grabbing visual media? Yet over two hundred years ago, the poet William Wordsworth found similar challenges in a pre-Electronic Age, as he tried to flee literary distractions and espoused the value of spending time alone in nature:

THE TABLES TURNED
UP! up! my Friend, and quit your books;
Or surely you'll grow double:
Up! up! my Friend, and clear your looks;
Why all this toil and trouble?

The sun, above the mountain's head,
A freshening lustre mellow
Through all the long green fields has spread,
His first sweet evening yellow.

Enough of Science and of Art;
Close up those barren leaves;
Come forth, and bring with you a heart
That watches and receives.

Find solitude to reduce external distractions, then engage your senses and your mind by allowing the beauty of creation to become visible and draw you to the Creator.

Engaging the Spirit: The Discipline of Meditation

Though it's mentioned many times in the Bible and featured prominently in the psalms, meditation is too often an overlooked aspect of contemporary Christian faith. Christian meditation does not seek to empty the mind on the path to enlightenment; instead it focuses on ridding our minds of distractions so that we can fill them with the knowledge of the fullness of God's love (see Ephesians 3:17–19). Without distractions, we can fill our minds with truth so that a spiritual transformation can occur.

So what should we meditate on as we sit in God's creation with our eyes open? How about these words:

> Worship him who made the heavens, the earth, the sea and the springs of water. (Revelation 14:7)

Or Psalm 29, which begins with these words:

> Give honor to the LORD, you angels;
>> give honor to the LORD for his glory and strength.
> Give honor to the LORD for the glory of his name.
>> Worship the LORD in the splendor of his holiness.
>>> (verses 1–2, NLT)

The psalm goes on to describe how God's presence is visible in lightning, thunder, trees, mountains, desert, and waters.

Psalm 104 is another great passage. This is the ecology psalm. In incredible detail, the psalmist connects the dots between all the various parts of the global ecological system while recognizing the beginning and end of all life as the great Creator. The psalmist describes the atmosphere, geology, water cycles, and all life forms in terms of their relationships to one another and to God.

Water issues from springs and runs down from the mountains to quench the thirst of all animals, while watering giant trees and fields along the way. Grass grows for cattle and other beasts of the field. Man can cultivate domestic crops for himself, even "wine that gladdens the heart of man" (verse 15). Whereas the proper habitat for livestock is low-lying fields, the proper habitat for mountain goats is, well, mountains. Storks need pine trees, hyraxes need rocky crags, and whales need the ocean. Man goes out to his work every day, and predators come out at night. Everything works, there's no pollution, and all God's creatures have what they need for life.

> O LORD, what a variety of things you have made!
>> In wisdom you have made them all.
>> The earth is full of your creatures....
> May the glory of the LORD last forever!
> The LORD rejoices in all he has made! (Psalm 104:24, 31, NLT)

As we meditate on the phenomenal gifts we have been given—salvation and creation—we will be as helpless to restrain our worship as the psalmist.

Using Our Hands: Worshiping Through Re-Creation

Our culture is almost obsessed with recreation. We love to play, to get away from it all. We love the activities of recreation, and we love the toys that come with it: boats, ATVs, motor homes, skis, snowmobiles. We love to play in neighborhood parks, amusement parks, national parks, and Fenway Park. But no matter how much fun we have playing, we have to admit that it's hardly transformational.

God offers a different intensity of experience—re-creation instead of recreation. He presents us with opportunities to put our faith into action and to worship Him in the process. His offer is both fun and transformational; we can be part of something larger than ourselves for the benefit of others. Part of that transformation may be calling us to consider new patterns of living that better steward the garden.

Perhaps the Creator will urge you to get involved in a local community group that restores a degraded natural area. Maybe you'll find yourself some Saturday morning pulling up kudzu, planting trees in a blighted neighborhood, or picking up litter along the beach. Maybe you'll find yourself walking more, eating less, or buying local. Whatever the specifics, you can be sure that God will be in it, working to transform you, and He will give you opportunities to take your enthusiasm for His creation and turn it into actions.

As you make changes in your lifestyle that help the creation, you will find that these choices bring you closer to our Creator and your fellow earth dwellers. You'll see that these choices have benefits for people as well as for the rest of creation. Although the issues are complex and the world is big, the planet's health improves as each of us makes our small contributions. The interconnectedness of all things allows one small act in our backyard to improve the lives of our brothers or sisters living halfway around the world and for generations to come.

By choosing to give up a Saturday to clean up a local stream, you make an investment that will benefit your unborn grandkids. By buying fair-trade coffee, you help raise the standard of living for a coffee farmer in Guatemala. By buying locally grown vegetables, you help a local farmer survive in the age of industrialized agriculture. By using less gasoline, you reduce the likelihood that some of Alaska's pristine wilderness will be fouled by an oil spill, and help preserve creation's ability to support your Eskimo brothers and sisters. The list of benefits is long.

We all live practically, day by day, and these types of activities give us a chance to take intangible motivations and convert them into tangible acts of stewardship. We can put on our bib overalls and become real gardeners of Eden. We can get our hands dirty and receive the satisfaction that comes with a job well done. But our satisfaction should not end there. Our acts of sacrifice offer a huge spiritual reward as well. Our very acts of service can make a huge statement to the world that we are willing to sacrifice our own desires for the sake of the entire creation.

Imagine the power of a multitude of faithful people who join together to say:

This world is a gift from God.

We want to pass it on to future generations in better condition than we received it.

To accomplish this, we are willing to make personal sacrifices.

And what if that multitude of people, joined together across social, economic, racial, and political lines, actually began to *do something together*? What if they didn't wait for the government to enact new laws and regulations and went ahead and decreased their use of fossil fuels? What if they didn't complain about the giant agribusinesses growing genetically modified crops and instead went to their local farmers' market and bought food from people in their own community? What if they didn't wait for the government to clean up a polluted site but organized their neighbors and cleaned it up themselves?

We are talking about a completely grass-roots, green, anti-revolution, based not in a desire for power but in a desire to please the Creator. Driven by humility and the desire to serve. A revolution of gardeners.

Can you imagine such a movement? Could you sign on to such a movement? Are you willing to prayerfully consider this?

If you did this—if *we* all did this—don't you think the world would be transformed? Consider how this movement might realize the words of the apostle Paul:

> Because of the service by which you have proved yourselves, men will praise God for the obedience that accompanies your confession of the gospel of Christ, and for your generosity in sharing with them and with everyone else. (2 Corinthians 9:13)

I would love to be part of this kind of movement—local, humble, loving. Using our eyes, minds, spirit, and hands together in community, we could demonstrate sacrificial love that would draw people to understand more of their world, themselves, and their Creator.

What do you say? Let's become a revolution of gardeners.

8

Creation Care as Compassion

If you have men who will exclude any
of God's creatures from the shelter of compassion
and pity, you will have men who will deal
likewise with their fellow men.

—SAINT FRANCIS OF ASSISI

Biblical orthodoxy without compassion
is surely the ugliest thing in the world.

—FRANCIS SCHAEFFER

A revolution of gardeners. Motivated by our profound sense of gratitude to the Creator, and embracing our solemn responsibility to care for the creation, we understand that our daily sacrifices are our spiritual act of worship (see Romans 12:1).

Creation care comes with another motivation as well: to show compassion to our brothers and sisters. There is an intersection between these two responsibilities. As we care for the creation, people benefit.

As I sit here looking out my window, it's hard for me to see the effect of environmental degradation on others. After all, my friends and family are not experiencing any effects of pollution. Or so I believe. The stories I hear on the radio or read on the Internet are impersonal and don't seem urgent. It's often difficult to see the connection between my choices and the welfare of others. I know there's a connection, but it can be difficult to act on that conviction without seeing it for myself.

Toward that end, consider these examples that point out the incredible connections between our choices and others' daily lives.

Africa

The Niger Delta was one of the most fertile coastal areas in the world. This Eden of five million acres was formed where the Niger River meets the Gulf of Guinea on the western coast of Africa. Here were coastal salt marshes, mangrove swamps, tropical rain forests, and rich farmland. It was a natural wonderland, filled with animals and clean water teeming with fish. The Ogoni people were one of several tribes that lived in the Delta region. They weren't rich, but they were able to feed themselves well from the bounty of fish and plants in the Delta.

But in 1956, unlimited riches were discovered in the form of oil and the end of the Ogoni prosperity began. Nigeria was still a British colony at the time; independence would come four years later, in the same year John F. Kennedy was elected president of the United States.

Representatives from the world's major oil companies swooped in to extract as much of the oil as possible: Royal Dutch Shell, France's Total, Italy's Agip, ExxonMobil, and Chevron. These were not bad people; they were simply treasure hunters, and buried treasure had been discovered. The objective was to recover the treasure, whatever the cost. They knew that modern treasure hunting required one key strategy— pay the government handsomely for the rights to conduct your exploration. And pay they did, to the tune of more than half of the profits from the venture. In 2005, this amounted to payments in excess of $60 billion. However, virtually none of these payments ever reached the Ogoni people.

The environmental effects of the industry have far outstripped the benefits to local villagers. Since 1976, over 100 million gallons of oil have been spilled across the land, water, and forests of the area. Underground aquifers used for drinking water have been contaminated. Farmland has been ruined.

In 1998, a river caught fire. The river of gasoline was formed when a pipeline valve malfunctioned. Tragically, massive numbers of people were in the river when it ignited. Over a thousand people burned to death, and the fire kept burning for over two weeks.

The bountiful fish of the past are gone. Marine life has been decimated to the point that the locals now must import nearly all their food and eat frozen fish, if they are wealthy enough to afford it, which most are not since a single piece of frozen fish is equal to a day's wage for most delta residents.

Hundreds of flares have been burning off unwanted natural gas for decades, resulting in caustic acid rain and the release of millions of pounds of greenhouse gases. The acid rain has corroded metals, ruined crops, and caused respiratory and other health problems for the people of the region.

Hundreds of acres of the rich mangrove forest have been clear-cut to make room for the oil extraction infrastructure. Ironically, Nigeria must import most of its oil since its refineries are seldom operational. Most villages in the Delta do not have power or access to clean water. And all of this in spite of Nigeria being the world's sixth largest oil exporter.

There has been one more parting gift left by the oil companies— civil war. Decades of frustration with a government that siphoned off virtually all of the oil revenue and left local people with nothing has prompted widespread revolt. Kidnapping of oil workers for ransom is common and is seen as the only way to realize direct benefits from the oil trade.

After the past fifty years, most Nigerians in the area wish that their oil had never been discovered. Many of them are Christians longing to go back to the days of peaceful fishing and farming.

It could be easy to feel detached from this story as we sit in our comfortable American homes. But as Felix James Harry, a husband, father of two, and fisherman will tell you, even a man of strong faith like him can feel discouraged by the situation. "We can hardly catch fish anymore," he says. "Surviving is very hard." Yet Felix has faith that the God who loves him will sustain him and his family. "He is my refuge and my fortress," he states emphatically.[1]

There is plenty of blame to go around. We can point to the oil companies, the corrupt Nigerian government, or the lawless rebels. Or perhaps our fingers should even point to ourselves, realizing that the greater our demand for a finite resource, the greater the lengths people will go to supply that demand.

Appalachia

"My father was a coal miner. I had three brothers was coal miners. We worked a total of probably approximately two hundred years among us."

Jim Foster has lived his entire life at the Y&O Coal Camp, outside of Charleston, West Virginia. "We needed the coal to produce electricity and stuff our nation needs. But I believe they could mine it better without destroying the environment like they are doing with mountaintop removal."

Jim is one of thousands of self-described "mountain people" in West Virginia, Tennessee, and Kentucky who have seen the land around them decimated by this new trend in coal mining—mountaintop removal, or MTR.

"I'm proud my dad didn't live to see this mountaintop removal, because if he had, he would absolutely…it would have broke his heart."

---

1. Tom O'Neill, "Curse of the Black Gold: Hope and Betrayal in the Niger Delta," *National Geographic*, February 2007.

Jesus once said that if we had faith as small as the seed of a mustard plant, we would be able to tell a mountain to move and it would comply. As it turns out, if you don't have faith, dynamite and heavy machinery will suffice.

MTR is among the latest ways to extract coal from the ground. Rather than following seams of coal deep into the ground with mine shafts, tops of mountains are completely blown off and scraped away to reach coal seams, sometimes hundreds of feet below the summit. This, of course, means that the soil and rock that once formed the mountain must be pushed off the top into the surrounding "hollers." As of 2006, over 1,200 miles of streams and rivers had been completely buried and 400,000 acres of pristine Appalachian forest had been leveled.

"When I grew up," continues Jim, "I could go anywhere I wanted to and fish any of the streams. Plenty of fish in it, plenty of wildlife, plenty of game to hunt for." But that has all changed. "Since they've started this strip mining and mountaintop removal, all the slides and stuff comin' off the mountains goes right into the river. It's got the riverbeds all filled up. The fish is all gone."

There are other costs as well. MTR mining depends on dynamite and machinery, not working men and women, for its success. "They don't want to pay men a decent wage to mine the coal," Jim complains. Rather than hiring people with living wage jobs, MTR replaces people with explosives and equipment. And the bills for environmental and economic destruction are paid by the mountain people.

Maria Gunnoe, from Boone County, West Virginia, has faced these costs personally. Since MTR moved onto land adjacent to hers in the year 2000, she's "lost two access bridges, the use of my water, and five acres of land." She continues, "There's thirteen landslides between me and the toe of the landfill behind me. Each time it rains, these landslides move…sometimes as much as five feet in one day." Since 2000, Maria's house has been flooded seven times due to the filling of stream channels caused by the nearby MTR. She has lost both land and water.

"Everyone downstream from where that mountaintop removal site is gets flooded and their wells are contaminated. My well is contaminated. Can't drink my water. I buy on average about $250 worth of water a month."

Once, after one of the floods washed five acres of her land away, Maria called a coal company engineer to come look at the damage caused by their MTR earthmoving. The engineer denied responsibility, calling it "an act of God."

"You know, the night when this wall of water was comin' down through the hollow at me, I run to the mountain. But the mountain was slidin' and I couldn't go there. I couldn't get out, the streams had me and my family surrounded. I literally hit my knees, and I prayed for everything I was worth! And there *was* an act of God that took place that night. But not the one they claimed." Maria and her family were miraculously spared from being washed away.

In 1972, others were not so fortunate. Strip mining caused the infamous Buffalo Creek Flood nearby in West Virginia. Though Buffalo Mining officials were concerned about the stability of an earthen dam created by mining activities, the residents below the dam were never warned. The rains continued to fall, and the dam gave way. The twenty-foot wall of water raged down through the ravine, and in a few minutes, 118 people were dead, 1,100 were injured, and 4,000 were homeless. An act of God? Or man's failure to adequately care for the garden?

In 2007, a coalition of church groups came together to issue a "Statement on Mountain Top Removal." Included were the following words:

As people of faith, called upon by our covenant with God and each other to safeguard and care deeply for what God has created, we cannot stand by while our mountains are being devastated.... Irresponsible mining practices damage the environment, hurt businesses based on tourism and the natural beauty of the state.... Genesis 1:31 tells us that God looked at everything God had made and found it very good. In obedience, we are obligated to care for God's wondrous creation that we may one day walk with God in the garden without shame.[2]

135

Maria reflected on her parents, grandparents, and great-grandparents who flourished in the lush Appalachian Mountains. "They loved this land and tended this land. It's land that wasn't meant to be developed. God put it way up high so they'd leave it alone. I've had people tell me that God put the coal there for us to mine. I have to disagree with that. He buried it because it's so daggone nasty!"

Both Maria and Jim remember the way it was before MTR arrived on the scene—a garden of Eden. Clean water, fish, wildlife, forests, and beauty as far as the eye could see. No wonder people disappeared into the mountains and carved out their own lives surrounded by such a glorious part of creation. "If it come down to it," Maria remarked, "we could live up under a rock cliff with what the good Lord above give us. And we could *live* like that, as long as we got clean water, clean air, and a healthy environment. We can take care of ourselves from there. But when they contaminate our water, our air, and our environment, we're gonna die no matter what we do. That's it."[3]

---

2. "Statement on Mountain Top Removal," West Virginia Council of Churches, Charleston, West Virginia, September 2007, www.wvcc.org.

3. "Like Walking Onto Another Planet," stories compiled by Carol Warren, Ohio Valley Environmental Coalition, Huntington, West Virginia.

Central America

Coffee is biofuel for humans. Trailing only oil, coffee is the second-largest commodity traded in the world. It is grown in forty-nine countries, employing an estimated 25 million coffee farmers.

But the growing and harvesting of coffee causes significant environmental and economic challenges. On the environmental front, traditional agricultural practices have devastated the rain forests of Central America. Coffee plants grow naturally in the highly diverse tropical rain forest where they are sheltered from the hot sun by the other trees that make up the forest canopy. However, the farming technique of choice has been "slash and burn," which wipes out large tracts of rain forest to create coffee plantations. Coffee plants don't really like growing in the full sun. To compensate for less than optimal conditions and to increase the yield of coffee berries, most growers pump the soil with synthetic chemical fertilizers. When the rainy season arrives, rainwater carries soil—and chemicals—from these fields in hilly upland regions into surrounding streams, rivers, and lakes. Both the soil erosion uphill and the deposits of chemicals downhill cause environmental damage.

Felipe Castro is a coffee farmer whose fields perch on the edge of what many people consider the most beautiful lake in the world, Lake Atitlán, in southwest Guatemala. With his wife, Marbila, a daughter, and two sons, he makes his home in San Lucas Toliman, surrounded by three volcanoes and a mile above sea level. Today, about 12,000 people live in San Lucas Toliman, and another 10,000 live in the surrounding rural area.

The rich volcanic soil and moderate climate make these mountain slopes an ideal place to grow a variety of crops, particularly coffee.

Once the center of Mayan civilization, this area of Guatemala has been growing coffee since the early 1700s. But growing coffee is a tricky business.

For one thing, prices are very volatile. In May 1998 the price Guatemalan coffee farmers got for a pound of beans was $1.47. Three months later, prices had dropped nearly in half, to $0.81 per pound. Prices continued to plummet, bottoming out at $0.36 per pound in November 2003. With middlemen, called "coyotes," taking a large cut of their profits, most small growers found that they couldn't cover the cost of growing the beans. Large-scale coffee growers plowed under their coffee plants and planted sugarcane instead. Many small growers left their fields and migrated north to find jobs. "The fall in coffee prices made it really difficult to look after my family and educate my children," remembers Felipe.

Others stayed and organized themselves into cooperatives. Felipe believed that his Mayan heritage and familiarity with native plants could play a role in protecting the environment while, at the same time, providing a living wage. He convinced several fellow small growers in San Lucas Toliman to band together to take advantage of the area's reputation as the source of some of the world's best coffee as a means to get higher return for their labor. "One of my main aims is to compete in the markets on quality instead of quantity," he told his fellow growers.

In a culture where the independence of the individual is prized, knitting together a coalition of farmers who have seen each other as competitors is one of Felipe's most impressive accomplishments. Today, Asociación Ijatz includes fifty-eight coffee growers and twenty-eight other local small businesses.

Felipe is a buzz saw of activity. He has led an effort to promote composting to encourage coffee growers to switch from conventional fertilizers to organic. He has shown the wisdom of growing his coffee plants in shade provided by dozens of other species of native trees. "If we grow trees in shade," Felipe explains, "there will not be soil erosion, and we can use compost to help them grow. We also help save threatened native plants." [4]

Co-ops such as Asociación Ijatz are critical to the survival of people like Felipe. But they are only half of the equation.

Many people have discovered the plight of coffee growers like Felipe. Organizations and importers such as Sustainable Harvest (www.sustainableharvest.com), Equal Exchange (www.equalexchange.com), and Kapeh-Utz (www.kapeh-utz.com) grew out of a desire to protect the environment while ensuring farmers are compensated fairly. These companies and others launched fair-trade coffee.

Fair-trade coffee means that coffee growers are guaranteed a minimum price for their coffee, regardless of world commodity prices at the time of sale. Currently, the price paid to organic farmers is about $1.50 per pound. The guaranteed minimum price can accomplish much in the lives of farmers like Felipe. Written over sixty years ago, the words of Andrés Uribe, author of the book *Brown Gold,* ring true today:

> "We in Latin America have a task before us which is staggering to the imagination—illiteracy to be eliminated, disease to be wiped out, good health to be restored, a sound program of nutrition to be worked out for millions of people. The key to all of this… is an equitable price for coffee." If they could secure a

---

4. "Felipe Miza Castro–Coffee Farmer," The Fairtrade Foundation, www.fairtrade.org.uk/producers/coffee/felipe_miza_castro.aspx.

fair price, they could work a "miracle" similar to the thriving United States. "If coffee cannot receive an equitable price, then you cast these millions of persons loose to drift in a perilous sea of poverty and privation, subject to every chilling wind, every subversive blast."[5]

A couple of years ago, Kansan John Fawcett traveled to Guatemala as part of a group looking for infrastructure projects to help fund. While there, John met Felipe Castro and was moved by Felipe's passion to help his people and the environment. "The coffee farmers of the area work so hard and don't make much money," John recounts. "They are battling for things that are right. They want to develop farms that are sustainable and can be passed down from one generation to the next." John decided that he wanted to try to do something to help.

He started Kapeh-Utz (pronounced "capé ootz") to accomplish something unusual in this age of global agribusiness: "to buy direct from a group of people."

His business plan? "Profit will follow, if you don't worry about profit."

His mission statement? "Coffee With a Cause."

His motivation? "God has called everyone who He has blessed with an abundant life to bless those that are less fortunate."

John sees this as his chance to do that, while also being a good steward of the creation.

As Felipe said, "If you buy our coffee, it will result in protecting the environment, especially our beautiful lake." He pauses momentarily.

---

5. Andrés Uribe, quoted in Mark Pendergrast, *Uncommon Grounds* (New York: Basic Books, 1999), 238.

"We will also get better pay for our labor," and echoing the dreams of parents the world over, he adds, "and this will mean that our children can go to school and get an education."

• • •

Hearing these stories, we realize that global warming is not the only reason to reconsider our dependence on coal, oil, and other non-renewable resources. We can begin to see that choices we make affect others. People's lives and livelihoods are at stake.

140

Jesus Himself established the model for us: "I have compassion for these people," He said before He fed the four thousand (Matthew 15:32). As we tend the garden, we also are moved to help our fellow gardeners with love and compassion. Both our worship of the Creator and our compassion toward His children compel us to care for creation.

Part II

Becoming
a Gardener

Introduction

As I walked through the grocery store parking lot a while ago, a car's bumper sticker caught my attention:

GOD'S ORIGINAL PLAN WAS TO HANG OUT IN A GARDEN
WITH SOME NAKED VEGETARIANS

After laughing out loud, I thought about this statement for a while longer. Today, this simple idea has become wedged in my consciousness. Most of our lives are so different from the idyllic, carefree lifestyle this phrase suggests. Once we have a career or a family, we no longer "hang out." Instead, we rush from one place to another on a tight schedule, juggling careers, family, finances, and faith. A tremendous amount of our attention and resources are spent on what we wear and what we eat. And though we aren't all naked vegetarians, we still don't have much to show for ourselves. As we know, affluence and materialism are not good hedges against discontent, depression, or destruction.

So I think it's time for us to return to God's original plan: God and mankind together in the garden. There was meaningful work in taking care of the garden and seeing that its great diversity flourished. Joy and peace were ours if we fulfilled our duties. And all was right with the world. Of course, that was a long time ago, and the world is completely different now. Can that original idea still apply?

In many ways, yes, I believe it can. We do still live in a garden, one that's planetary rather than a single garden plot. But as we've seen in earlier chapters, the commandment to steward the garden is as relevant today as in Adam and Eve's day. And the Master Gardener is still available for free consultations at any time.

Once we're convinced we should live differently and we want to become gardeners of Eden, it's time for the action side of the equation. Maybe you've decided to decrease your impact or simply try to do better. That's great. What specific actions you should take next will depend on your starting place. There are many practical ways to translate your convictions into actions, which is why I've included fifty gardening tips in the next few chapters to help you come up with a to-do list. As I mentioned earlier, the two most common questions I'm asked are "Who should I believe?" and "What should I do?" Based on my years of personal experience and research, this section is my answer to the second question.

This isn't an exhaustive list; it's a beginning point. If your interest is piqued in one area or another, you'll have no trouble finding more comprehensive discussions and lists of items at related Web sites, on blogs, in magazine articles, and other resources listed in the back of the book. I've included my favorite information sources here for you to explore and generate ideas of your own.

The gardening tips come in four major categories:

- Food
- Energy
- Transportation
- Home

In each category, you'll find Gardening Principles to guide the individual Gardening Tips. The tips are listed from easier-to-implement to more challenging, many with sources for additional information.

As you become a more adept gardener, you may want to come back and consider some of the more advanced methods here. But my main goal with offering these tips is to help you consider your role as a gardener and encourage you to find ideas that are as fun and rewarding as those I've found. Remember, gardening Eden does *not* have to be a burden. I trust you will find these tips a step toward proving that.

145

9

Food in the Garden

To live, we must daily break the body and shed the blood of Creation. When we do this knowingly, lovingly, skillfully, reverently, it is a sacrament. When we do it ignorantly, greedily, clumsily, destructively, it is a desecration. In such desecration we condemn ourselves to spiritual and moral loneliness, and others to want.

—WENDELL BERRY, *The Gift of Good Land*

What is more basic to human life than food? Throughout human history, the hunting, growing, collecting, cooking, and eating of food have been key factors in creating cultural identity. It is so fundamental to the human experience that the Bible is filled with stories that use food to communicate deep spiritual truths. Jesus's first miracle was turning water into wine (see John 2:7–10). Jesus told us that He is the bread of life (see John 6:35). The Jews were spared the angel of death and instructed to remember God's protection by eating a Passover meal of roasted lamb, bitter herbs, and unleavened bread (see Exodus 12:8). The apostle Paul explained sin by saying it was like a tiny bit of yeast that affected the whole batch of dough (see 1 Corinthians 5:6–8). Eating a meal together was a symbol of a deep commitment to one another (see Genesis 31:54; Psalm 41:9). David wrote that experiencing God is like being at a banquet table that He has prepared for us (see Psalm 23:5).

Do our lives recognize and celebrate the spiritual symbolism of food? Should we really "think outside the bun" so that we can "have it our way"? Are you "lovin' it," or are you left asking, "Where's the beef?" As we drive through the processed food joint on our way to our next family activity—ingesting calories in the quickest way possible—are we missing the opportunity to celebrate God's bounty in a meaningful way?

More and more people are noticing that we are missing some of the richness found in the lives of our grandparents, whose lives were lived, to a large extent, around the dinner table. In fact, an entire international movement has sprung up. The Slow Food USA movement was founded twenty years ago to "counteract fast food and fast life, the disappearance of local food traditions, and people's dwindling interest in the food they eat, where it comes from, how it tastes, and how our food choices affect the rest of the world."[1]

As people of faith, we can find at the dinner table a time-honored place to connect with the Creator/Provider of all we have and with the family members we love. How can we do this in ways that help sustain the planet at the same time? There are three main Gardening Principles having to do with food that we can use to better steward this creation we have been given:

- Eat Local
- Eat Healthy
- Eat Your Own

Gardening Principle: Eat Local

Most people haven't a clue about how healthy or unhealthy our food is. Most of us don't even know which continent it came from.

According to the 2000 census, approximately 80 percent of us live in urban areas; that means most of us are rather disconnected from our food sources. At the same time, the agricultural industry has under-

1. www.slowfoodusa.org.

gone a massive reengineering. In the last third of the twentieth century, small family farms were consolidated into larger corporate agribusinesses. With this consolidation came a great increase in farm productivity, fueled in part by the injection of the new farming steroids: chemical fertilizers, pesticides, mechanization, and genetic engineering. The increased productivity helped drive prices down to the point where most family farmers could no longer compete.

Further, in the past twenty years, we have seen a new agriculture phenomenon: the globalization of the food supply. One hundred years ago, most food was grown within one hundred miles of a person's dinner table. Fifty years ago, transportation advances began a revolution. We could get food grown in other parts of the country—oranges from California and Florida, cheese from Wisconsin, cherries from Oregon, beef from Texas, salmon from Alaska. Today, in the early days of the twenty-first century, our food comes from all over the planet. In the dead of winter, we can get fresh grapes from Chile, asparagus from Peru, and tomatoes from Mexico. Consider green onions as an example of the globalization of food. In 1982, 73 percent of the green onions consumed in the United States was grown domestically, and 27 percent came from Mexico. Twenty five years later, in 2007, the United States grew only 6 percent of the green onions we ate. The remaining 94 percent was grown in Mexico.

In 2007, nearly one-fourth of all the fresh fruits and vegetables in our stores came from outside our borders. About half of all tree nuts grew on trees in foreign countries, and a whopping two-thirds of fish and shellfish came from outside our country. Why? The competitive marketplace is a powerful thing, and it responds quickly to the desires of consumers. We've come to expect the availability of foods that are out of season where we live. We want fresh produce in the wintertime. So the Southern Hemisphere has been more than happy to oblige.

Gardening Tip 1: Consider the Impacts of Transportation on Food Purchases

We import Peruvian asparagus. We export California lettuce. Everyone wins, right? Maybe not. Today, we're only starting to realize the impacts of a global economy on the planet. A recent study looked at the environmental costs of shipping lettuce grown in California to England. Every food calorie the lettuce provides in England costs 127 calories of fuel to transport it there.

Some studies have suggested that if we were forced to pay the real environmental costs of transporting food, our grocery bills would increase by 12 percent. The distance even food grown right here in the United States has traveled has increased by 22 percent in the past twenty-five years. Now the average trip for fruits and vegetables from farm to fork is 1,500 miles. Each of those 1,500 miles requires the power by fossil fuels, resulting in impacts on the environment and to our deteriorating national infrastructure. Fully one-fifth of all petroleum products burned in the United States goes to transport our food. When we buy food grown locally, we save fuel, reduce pollution, and reduce wear and tear on our highways.

The importance of transportation can even outweigh other environmental concerns. Some studies have shown that the environment is better off if you buy conventionally produced local food than if you buy organic food that has to be transported one or two thousand miles to you. Of course, buying local *and* organic is a true win-win.

Gardening Tip 2: Become Concerned About Food Quality and Health

The United States and the European Union have strict environmental regulations on the food industry, from farm to store. What happens in foreign countries, however, is less certain. In 2007 in one month alone, the FDA detained nearly 850 shipments of food products coming into the United States. The food included fresh ginger containing pesticides, catfish contaminated with illegal drugs, and melon seeds laced with a toxin known to cause cancer. And that is just what was discovered in a tiny fraction of shipments, since the United States allows nearly 98.7 percent of all food shipments in *without* any type of inspection. We know that pet food poisoned with contaminated wheat gluten from China was severe enough to kill over one hundred dogs in 2005, but what have we ingested unknowingly? Back when we grew our own food, or at least purchased it from our neighbor, we could be fairly certain of the agricultural practices.

Today, some grocery stores provide for their customers country-of-origin information for meat, fish, cheese, produce, and other items. This does little to help ensure safety, so as you become aware of the countries of origin that have had the most problems with food safety issues, it's also good to work toward the following tips.

Gardening Tip 3: Visit Your Local Farmers' Market

Another way to support local farmers is to become a regular customer of nearby farmers' markets. Although definitions and regulations vary from one community to another, a farmers' market is generally a place where local growers sell their produce, meat, and other products directly to customers. Farmers' markets differ from individual produce stands in that multiple growers and producers are represented. In 1977, there were seven farmers' markets in the United States. In 2007, the United States Department of Agriculture estimated that more than 4,500 separate community-based farmers' markets were operating in this country. Obviously, the idea of buying local has become a movement. If you are wondering how to find the nearest farmers' market, a terrific online national directory can be found at www.farmersmarket.com.

And here's another benefit of a farmers' market that you might not think about. Most are held in downtown areas, often on weekends. With more and more people fleeing downtown areas, living in suburbs, and shopping in big retail complexes, farmers' markets bring something critical to the economic survival of all businesses in downtown areas—foot traffic. Many downtowns are complete ghost towns on the weekend. While you are buying your lettuce, beets, and cheese from a local grower, you are more likely to stop into the locally owned coffee shop or jewelry store or tailor and give those folks your business. Your ties to your community become even stronger in the process.

Gardening Tip 4: Shop at Local Farms

There are several ways you can help support local farmers. First, you can find nearby farms that offer "you pick" or seasonal produce stands. Ever since we moved from Southern California to Portland in 1985, we've been big fans of the Pumpkin Patch on Sauvie Island, which is located in the Columbia River just a few miles north of Portland. The Pumpkin Patch has grown from being a farm-based produce stand to a significant regional destination for locals and tourists alike. Here, the one million residents of the Portland metropolitan area come to experience one of many working family farms in the region. Blueberries, corn, beans, honey, jams, crafts, hay rides, a corn maze, and the big red barn full of farm animals draw huge summertime crowds.

No matter where you live, a real farm like the Pumpkin Patch is nearby and needs your support to survive in this world of giant corporate agribusinesses.

Gardening Tip 5: Join a CSA (Community Supported Agriculture)

CSAs are a type of food cooperative that allows customers to purchase shares of produce grown at a nearby farm. The farms are sometimes known as "subscription farms." The fruits and vegetables vary through-out the growing season, and a share usually provides enough fresh pro-duce for a family of four. Depending on the length of the growing season where you live, CSAs can provide weekly food shares for twenty or more weeks a year. Some CSAs offer fresh eggs, milk, and flowers as well. Most CSAs require you to go to a particular place each week to pick up your shares, but a few also offer delivery service. Many, but not all, CSAs offer food grown organically. It is important to research the farm, the farmer, and the products. Word of mouth speaks volumes here.

As Michael Pollan states eloquently in his bestseller *The Omnivore's Dilemma:*

> Of course, just because food is local doesn't necessarily mean it will be organic or even sustainable. There's nothing to stop a local farmer from using chemicals or abusing animals—except the gaze or good word of his customers. Instead of looking at labels, the local food customer will look at the farm for himself, or look the farmer in the eye and ask him how he grows his crops or treats his animals.[2]

To find a CSA near you, visit www.localharvest.org/csa.

Gardening Tip 6: Become Part of a Local Food Community
More and more people are realizing that eating healthier does not just mean buying organic bagged spinach. It is an even better thing if you know the patch of ground where the spinach grew, as well as the spinach farmer who grew it. Wendell Berry captured the link when he

---

2. Michael Pollan, *The Ominivore's Dilemma* (New York: Penguin Group, 2006) 257–258.

said: "Eating…is…an agricultural act."[3] But in the age of global commerce and industrial agriculture, this concept seems quaint and completely out of touch. Or does it?

The antidote to anonymous food is to become a real member of a local community. It means to climb aboard the train heading back to the future, gathering steam in the United States and Europe today. This is not the "Peace Train" that Cat Stevens sang about in the 1970s, but it's close. This is the train of smaller is better than bigger, local is better than foreign, big problems are best solved by millions of small individual acts. Decentralization and local self-sufficiency are its credos.

We have a divine example of this type of change agent. Jesus Himself put His confidence in twelve ordinary Joes and several Janes—real men and women who would take His miracles and messages and change the world. Jesus didn't worry about changing the power structure of the times, though He could have overthrown the entire Roman army and the religious leaders of the day with a word. He didn't start a revolutionary movement—He founded a community.

Imagine yourself as part of a local community, living in relationship with other gardeners. We recognize that we should love our neighbor as ourselves. But how exactly are we to love our neighbor if we don't know him? And how are we to know him if we work far from where we live, drive home in isolation, stop by the local drive-through and pick up a few bags of genetically engineered food product for our dinner, pull into our garage, and escape anonymously into our warm and comfortable cocoon-like home?

The polar opposite of this cocooning lifestyle is to be engaged and

---

3. Wendell Berry, "The Pleasures of Eating" from *What Are People For?* (New York: North Point Press, 1990).

involved in our communities. To be in the world, but not of the world. To offer ourselves as living sacrifices; to be transformers, not conformers. To know the issues of our street, our neighborhood, our community. To help each other achieve our aspirations. To be different; to offer salt to the bland, light to the dark. To become active members of a community so that we can meet our neighbor, know our neighbor, love our neighbor.

Food offers us that opportunity. We can seek out people who have devoted their lives to feeding others. We can develop a relationship with these people and, in the process, reconnect with creation. We might find ourselves advocating for the preservation of farmland. We might volunteer to help share our produce with someone in need. In the process, we may even have a new appreciation for God's provision of both food and people in our lives.

And we might even get to meet a neighbor like David Shonk of Bumblebee Farm.

Growing up in the Portland suburb of Beaverton, Oregon, David never expected to become a farmer. Though his dad was heavily involved in a big local church, the family never even had a garden, much less a farm. But his maternal grandmother owned a large piece of property east of Portland, mostly in nursery stock.

A sociology and geography major at Portland State University, Dave became enamored with the effect that food had in building strong communities in various cultures. After he and Suzy married, they decided to make a big lifestyle change—to take over Grandma's farm. Friends and family thought that the Shonks' move to the farm was rather quaint, but secretly they longed for the day when Dave and Suzy would land "real" jobs.

It took five years just to get the property in shape; clearing blackberries, repairing equipment, rebuilding barns. Dave and Suzy had a solid plan, practical as any fourth-generation farmer—start small, work hard, and invest in the future. They considered themselves to be stewards of the land and treated it accordingly. By 2003, Bumblebee Farm was ready to start producing food for customers.

Today, Dave and Suzy have about two and a half acres in organic production, growing everything from arugula to zucchini. Bumblebee provides fresh vegetables for forty CSA members, plus the additional folks who stop in weekly at the Shonks' Twelve Mile Market. Because very little of their costs go to transporting the food they grow, they earn enough to support their family. The Shonks, in turn, take their proceeds and spend it at other local small businesses in the area.

Farmers are a philosophical lot, and Dave is cut from the same cloth. " 'Farmer' is a self-appointed title," Dave once told me, "one that requires hard work and a compassionate heart." Dave has learned that others see farming as a respectable profession, and people accord him the same level of trust that farmers have received for generations in all cultures. Seen as straight shooters and stable, farmers are rarely assumed to be corrupt or lacking initiative. As a matter of fact, nowadays when Dave Shonk goes to a party in the city, he is often the center of attention; everyone wants to meet "Farmer Dave."

I once asked Dave to define success. He thought for a moment and said, "Having respectful relationships with the soil, water, legacy, family, and society. And having a stable family life with Suzy and my two daughters, Zia and Gracy. That is success."

Don't settle for just buying food anonymously; being a faceless customer for giant agribusinesses. Instead, become part of a local food community—knowing where your food grows and who grows it. And in the process you may help support others who are striving to be gardeners of Eden.

Gardening Principle: Eat Healthy

Tobacco and Alcohol. These are two things that many people of faith avoid, because of their effect on health. A common scripture used to support this position is 1 Corinthians 3:16-17:

> Don't you know that you yourselves are God's temple and that God's Spirit lives in you? If anyone destroys God's temple, God will destroy him; for God's temple is sacred, and you are that temple.

For some reason, I am less likely to extend this admonition to the topic of food. Perhaps you share this weakness with me. In spite of overwhelming evidence that we are becoming a nation of overweight and underfit citizens, we have failed to recognize that what we eat affects the temple. In the United States today, eating has become one of the most difficult personal areas in which to practice discipline and restraint. And we can't just blame the "food industry"—an age-old victimization strategy—but push ourselves away from the table long enough to face our own gluttony. (How's that for a word that doesn't get much airtime in our society?) We want the doughnut.

There are some fairly simple strategies that we can adopt to increase the likelihood we'll feed the temple better. Cook. Plan. Eat less. Eat better.

Gardening Tip 7: Cook

What ever happened to cooking? I mean cooking, not zapping. The skill of taking raw ingredients and combining them in ways that result in delicious and healthy meals. It seems like a lost art. It appears we have forfeited this ability for the sake of speed and convenience. A

2004 study showed that Americans spend over half of their total food budget eating out.

My wife, Vicki, and I have had the great pleasure of helping to mentor newly married couples for many years. One of the interesting trends we've noticed is how few young people can actually cook. Many were raised in families that didn't value the dinner table. Parents didn't pass down cooking skills to the next generation. Consequently, cooking is an intimidating challenge to many young adults.

And as cooking goes, so goes eating. Pollan makes the connection between the two:

> A successful local food economy implies not only a new kind of
> food producer, but a new kind of eater as well, one who regards
> finding, preparing, and preserving food as one of the pleasures
> of life rather than a chore.[4]

One of the first steps to healthier eating is preparing your own food. You control the ingredients, the portion size, the way it is prepared. Although intimidating, cooking can be a great joy and give us a great sense of accomplishment. Remember Rebekah's words to her son Jacob? "Go out to the flock and bring me two choice young goats, so I can prepare some tasty food for your father, just the way he likes it" (Genesis 27:9).

I love to cook. On Mother's Day, I often prepare cioppino, a seafood stew, for Vicki. The process of cooking for someone else is a remarkable act of service. As I peel the shrimp, scrub the clams, and chop the vegetables, I think about how much she will enjoy the fruit of my labor. In the same way, when Vicki makes one of my favorite

160

---

4. Pollan, *The Ominivore's Dilemma*, 239.

dishes, I understand that she is not just trying to meet my minimum daily requirements for vitamins and calories. Rather, she is trying to express her love for me by pulling a Rebekah, making me something "just the way I like it." Cooking for another person conveys a bit more than picking up Chinese takeout on the way home—which, by the way, does not qualify as "bringing her food from afar," the accolade given the noble woman of Proverbs 31.

This past winter, Vicki and I took a French cooking class together. It was marvelous, putting us together with eight other people, with whom our sole common bond was that we were all "foodies." Under the demanding expectations of our chef, Robert Reynolds, we learned a wide variety of basic skills, from how to "take apart a chicken" to the formula for pot de crème. I couldn't help thinking that this would have been nice information thirty years ago! The things we learned gave us new confidence and a sense of adventure in the kitchen at home. As Vicki can attest, there is nothing quite so affirming as the successful preparation of a soufflé.

So trade processed foods for fresh food, packaged dinners for recipes, and burgers in the car for meals at the dinner table.

Gardening Tip 8: Eat Less

We Americans love to eat. You don't hear much anymore about gluttony, but perhaps we have become a nation of gluttons. You and I are consuming 20 percent more calories each day than we did in 1982. We're eating fifty-seven more pounds of meat per year than our parents and grandparents did in the 1950s. Whereas we each consumed less than half a pound of high fructose corn syrup per year in 1970, that number skyrocketed to more than forty-two pounds by 2004.

Those added calories have gone to our waists, contributing to soaring levels of obesity, Type 2 diabetes, and other food-related health problems. Obesity is defined as a body mass index (BMI) greater than 30. To determine your BMI, multiply your weight in pounds by 703 and then divide that sum by your height in inches squared. For example, if you weigh 180 pounds and are 5 feet 10 inches (or 70 inches) tall, you would multiply your weight of 180 by 703 for a total of 126,540. Then you would find the total of 70 times 70 to get the number of your height squared, which is 4,900. Dividing 126,540 by 4,900 would give you a BMI of 25.8. A BMI of 25 is classified as overweight, but not until a person has a BMI of 30 is that person considered obese.

A 2006 study by the Centers for Disease Control and Prevention and the U.S. Surgeon General concluded that nearly two-thirds of all adults in the United States are either overweight or obese. Obesity was responsible for approximately 112,000 deaths in 2000, and is now viewed as strong a factor in contracting cancer as smoking is. Gluttony kills.

Contrasting with our gluttony and obesity, 850 million people on the planet are suffering from malnutrition. An estimated 5 million children under the age of five will die from lack of adequate food this year. The issues are complex, with agricultural practices, climate, distribution, population, politics, and economics all part of the problem. However, we face an alarming dichotomy: we Americans are killing ourselves with too much food while others die from a lack of it. Two questions for people of faith are these: How do we steward the garden so that all of God's people have access to good food? And should I make any changes in my eating habits to benefit this temple or others?

Gardening Tip 9: Buy Organic

Back in the day, organic food was something purchased by college coeds in Eugene, Berkeley, or Amherst. It was hard to find organic foods, especially fresh produce, and anything organic was twice as expensive as conventional food.

The situation has changed since then. The marketplace has responded. As people have become increasingly concerned about pesticides, fertilizers, growth hormones, and other chemicals in their food, they have turned to organic food as a healthier alternative. Organic food has become big, big business.

But are organic food products better for the creation? Do they represent a better way to garden Eden?

Well, the answer may be surprising: it depends. There are two important questions to ask as you try to evaluate the purchase of organic food products:

- Where was it grown?
- How much processing has it received?

As mentioned earlier, a key factor in the eco-friendliness of food is the distance it has to travel from farm to fork. Though an organic farmer doesn't use petroleum-based chemicals on her carrot ranch, the carrots still have to find their way to your kitchen. Perhaps that farmer lives in your neighborhood and brings you a basket brimming with carrot tops. Grab them and enjoy every last one of them with no guilt. But this is an unlikely scenario.

More likely the carrots come to you via a series of internal combustion engines including tractors, small trucks, and big rigs. Nearly 80 percent of all energy used in agriculture goes to the transporting and processing of the product. The most energy-efficient mode of transportation—the railroad—has become increasingly scarce in the transportation of food products. So, although an organic farmer may use less energy on the farm than his conventional neighbor, he may use the same amount to get it from his farm to you.

This is why you may be better off buying a local carrot, grown conventionally, but only transported a few miles than an organic one that is shipped a thousand miles or more.

Are you buying fresh organic carrots or sliced carrots in an organic frozen dinner? The level of processing affects food's environmental impact. The carrots in the frozen dinner get shipped to a processing plant (or two), combined with other ingredients, cooked, mixed with preservatives, packaged, shipped to a distributor, and ultimately trucked to your grocery store. Each of these steps requires fuel, and some steps actually decrease the nutritional value of the carrots.

If transportation and processing are equal between organically and conventionally grown foods, organic foods are generally better for the environment. Organic farming methods don't add harmful pesticides and fertilizers to the soil. Erosion is minimized through higher amounts of organic material in the soil. Use of fossil fuels is reduced. The food doesn't carry hitchhiking chemicals into your metabolism. And studies are starting to show something very interesting—organic food may be significantly healthier for you. It's healthier not just because it contains less badness, but also because it contains more goodness.

A growing number of studies are shedding new light on the effect of chemicals on food production. First, the actual nutritional value of our fruits, vegetables, meat, and dairy products have been declining since the 1940s. This is partially caused by the effect that artificial fertilizers and hormones have on living organisms—they provide a burst of energy which causes a flush of rapid growth. However, this rapid growth also results in an increased amount of water stored in the plant or animal tissues. Consequently, the tissue contains more water and fewer natural antioxidants, called phytonutrients. On the other hand, plants and animals raised using organic processes are stronger, contain less water, and are filled with more vitamins. More goodness.

If you're living within a tight food budget and trying to decide which organic products are worth the additional expense, consider this: fruits and vegetables that have thin skins are more likely to carry pesticides and other chemical residues if grown conventionally. So it makes sense to spend a little extra for organic grapes, peaches, apples, strawberries, tomatoes, lettuce, celery, and bell peppers. Produce with thick skins such as bananas, melons, corn, pineapples, and avocados are more naturally protected from the chemical sprays.[5]

Gardening Principle: Eat Your Own

Can you remember the best tomato you ever ate? Was it an organic $3.00 tomato from Whole Foods? I'll bet not. I'm guessing it was one that came out of your grandmother's garden, or perhaps even your own. Want to be a gardener of Eden? Then garden. Wendell Berry puts it this way:

> Growing our own food, unlike buying it, is a complex activity, and it affects deeply the shape and value of our lives. We like the thought that the outdoor work that improves our health should produce food of excellent quality that, in turn, also improves and safeguards our health. We like no less the thought that the home production of food can improve the quality of family life. Not only do we intend to give our children better food than we can buy for them at the store, or than they will buy for themselves from vending machines or burger joints, we also know that growing and preparing food at home can

---

5. "Shopper's Guide to Pesticides in Produce," 5th Edition, Environmental Working Group, 2006, www.foodnews.org.

provide family work—work for everybody. And by thus elaborating household chores and obligations, we hope to strengthen the bonds of interest, loyalty, affection, and cooperation that keep families together.[6]

Although Mr. Berry eloquently describes some half dozen or more advantages to growing our own food, I'll add one more benefit—it is an intensely spiritual experience. It reminds us that there is a providential Creator who blesses us with sunshine, rain, and growth. There is no way you can weed a garden without considering the power of an uncontrolled habit to overtake and destroy a good life. And you understand that the invisible foundation for a fruitful garden—the soil—is critical to the fruitfulness of the plant. Jesus loved gardening analogies—including the parable of the sower and the soils—to illustrate our spiritual condition.

Gardening Tip 10: Grow a Garden

A wonderful passage written by the prophet Isaiah points out that there is a good way and a bad way to garden. In remarkable detail, the passage describes proper plowing techniques, where and how to plant seeds, harvesting regimens, and processing of crops. Then Isaiah summed up the righteous and successful farmer in this way:

> His God instructs him and teaches him the right way.... All this also comes from the LORD Almighty, wonderful in counsel and magnificent in wisdom. (Isaiah 28:26, 29)

---

6. Wendell Berry, *The Gift of Good Land* (New York: North Point Press, 1981), 155.

God wants it all done right. In our relationships with Him, in our relationships with our fellow gardeners, or in our relationships with the garden itself, it matters how we do it. And He is standing by, wanting to teach us and give us the wisdom we need to garden in a good way.

Maybe you have room in your own yard. Plant a garden. Maybe you live in an apartment with no room. Plant tomatoes in containers, or look for a nearby community garden. Maybe you can borrow some space from a nearby friend or relative. Maybe you can team up with a friend from church. Whatever it takes, get some dirt under your fingernails.

10

Energy in the Garden

The sun was like a great visiting presence that
stimulated and took its due from all animal energy.
When it flung wide its cloak and stepped down
over the edge of the fields at evening,
it left behind it a spent and exhausted world.

—WILLA CATHER, *One of Ours*

Energy is a bit of a conundrum.

We can *see* beauty. We can *taste* food. We can *feel* home. But though we're completely dependent on it, energy is for the most part an invisible commodity. We trade many things for it, but we don't ever touch it. Each time we flip on a switch, we trust that it will be there when we need it to mysteriously power our lives. We hear of the shocking price of barrels of oil, but we don't really *feel* that like we do when we hear that chicken breasts are selling for two dollars a pound.

But visible or not, the cost of energy hits us daily at the gas pump and in our electric bills. We know its rewards, but we're also vaguely aware that it comes with consequences. We know that the production of energy has environmental costs associated with it—air pollution, environmental degradation, dependency on foreign sources.

Though energy is a mysterious commodity, there is a very real and tangible benefit to reducing our energy use—it saves us money. And that is a powerful motivation. Whereas recycling, or buying organic, or planting trees are all good things to do, at the very least they are economically neutral, and in some cases, cost us extra. Energy is delightfully direct in comparison. Use less; pay less. Save more energy; save more money.

Three energy principles can help us evaluate our impact on both creation and our pocketbooks:

- Know how much energy you use.
- Reduce your use of energy.
- Use renewable energy sources.

Gardening Principle: Know How Much Energy You Use

Energy use in the United States can be imagined as a pie with four slices. The largest slice of the pie, representing nearly one-third of the total, is energy used by industry, which includes the manufacturing sector. The second largest section is transportation, which in 2006 represented about 28 percent of all energy use. The commercial sector uses about 18 percent of the total energy used for office, retail, and all other non-industry business. Our homes eat up the fourth slice of pie—21 percent of the total—in residential energy use.

Do you have any idea how much energy your house consumes?

Are you using more this year than last year?

Do you ever look at those little usage charts that many utility companies put on your bill to show your usage trends over the past year?

Are you doing things to help reduce your energy use such as shutting off lights, installing new weather stripping or storm windows, or sealing cracks around your fireplace?

Has that saved you any energy and money?

Jesus told a story about energy and the danger of running out of it. Remember the parable of the ten bridesmaids in Matthew 25? The ten women went out at night to meet the groom who was returning from a journey. They were going to escort him to a late-night wedding feast.

The torches that the women took with them most likely burned olive oil. Half of the women were wise enough to make sure they brought some extra oil along with them, but the other five didn't worry about it. After all, they were just going to be out a short time.

However, it got later and later, and the groom was a no-show. The women sat down to wait but soon fell asleep. Around midnight, the groom finally approached. The flustered women woke from their drowse and went to trim the wicks and relight the torches. Of course, the ones who had overlooked their energy need were stuck unprepared, so they had to leave the group to try to buy oil somewhere at midnight. Perhaps there was a twenty-four-hour convenience store nearby. While they were gone, the groom welcomed the five who had thought about their energy needs ahead of time into the wedding banquet. The other five were left out in the cold and the dark. The first oil crisis and an interesting lesson for us all.

Let's bring this back home to our day. In order for us to be good stewards of what we have, we need to be prepared. Though there is an "endless" supply of energy coming to our house, it still is our responsibility to know what we have, what we are likely to use, and to be good stewards of it. We are expected to count the cost (see Luke 14:28).

This is especially true since we know that every drop of crude oil or coal that is burned to create energy for our homes comes at a price to creation. The devastated coal country of West Virginia and Kentucky serves as an example that both man and the environment are called upon to pay a heavy cost. Men risk their lives daily a mile below the surface in deep tunnels or on the surface, leveling entire mountains. Here in the United States, more than half of all of our electrical power comes from the burning of coal, fouling both land and air.

Gardening Tip 11: Track Your Home Energy Usage

Energy is a miraculous and precious gift. If we valued energy the way we do other treasured resources—diamonds, for example—we wouldn't be cavalier about its misuse. The economics of energy are changing our perspective. As gasoline prices rise ever higher, we *are* starting to be more careful with how we use it. But we must also show that type of careful conservatism with other types of energy, giving thanks to the Creator for this precious and readily available resource. Like the wise bridesmaids who prepared for how much oil they might need, we have to be aware so we can prepare for the unexpected.

174

If you pulled out your energy bills from the past couple years and made a quick chart from January to December, what do you think you'd find? You might make a chart for each type of energy you use: electricity (measured in kilowatt-hours, kWh), natural gas (measured in therms), and heating oil (measured in gallons) to figure out the totals for each type of energy you use in a given year. You might use a spreadsheet program on your computer to see how your energy use changes over the course of a year. When I did this, I learned that our family was typical of most in the Northern Hemisphere. Our biggest energy months are December and January. Our family used about twice as much electricity in the long, cold, dark days of December than we did in the brighter days of May and June. We used nearly five times as much natural gas in the winter months than we did in the summer.

Knowing this helped me evaluate our energy use and take the first step toward positive change. From there, I was ready to move on to specific actions.

Gardening Tip 12: Calculate Your Carbon Footprint

As we talked about in chapter 5, the production of energy for our homes generates a great deal of carbon dioxide and other greenhouse gases. It is likely that these gases that come from our power plants and cars are at least partially responsible for global climate changes. We can estimate our personal impact on the formation of greenhouse gases by looking at our lifestyle choices, such as the size of our houses; the way we heat, light, and cool our homes; the type of cars we drive and how many miles we drive; and how much we fly. By measuring these and other factors, we can calculate our "carbon footprint"—our personal contribution to carbon in the atmosphere.

Several carbon footprint calculators are available on the Internet. The Climate Trust, a national nonprofit organization committed to helping reduce greenhouse gas emissions, sponsors one of the best. Their carbon calculator is available at www.carboncounter.org. It allows you to enter the actual amount of energy you use to heat and cool your home, the miles you drive with each car, and either the miles or hours you fly each year. It combines these to calculate your total emissions of greenhouse gases in tons per year. Finally, they allow you to purchase "carbon offsets," which help fund projects that reduce the impacts of the greenhouse gases you produce. These range from rain forest restoration projects to electrification of big-rig truck stops so that overnighting trucks can plug in for power to their cabs, rather than idling all night long.

The Rocky Mountain Institute has an excellent resource for calculating your household emissions. It is included in a terrific pamphlet called "Cool Citizens: Household Solutions," available at www.rmi.org/images/other/Climate/C02-12_CoolCitizensBrief.pdf.

The U.S. Environmental Protection Agency has an excellent "Personal Emissions Calculator" that gives you both your current "footprint" and steps you can take to reduce your energy use. This useful feature describes the likely effects of steps such as driving a more energy-efficient car, recycling, replacing incandescent light bulbs, adjusting your thermostat, and replacing old appliances. This calculator is available online at www.epa.gov/climatechange/emissions/ind _calculator.html.

Like the chart to calculate your home energy use, the carbon calculator is a helpful way to establish a benchmark and goals. Both help you to be a more responsible gardener of Eden, while avoiding the bridesmaids' dilemma—finding ourselves stuck without the needed energy.

In February of 2007, Vicki and I set a goal of reducing our carbon footprint by 20 percent in the coming year. We consciously tried to use less electricity at home, turned down the thermostat, and made some major changes in the way we drove our cars. Though we weren't fully successful in reaching our goal, we were able to reduce our overall footprint by more than 18 percent. Like trying to improve our personal spiritual lives, our economic condition, and our personal fitness, the key to success is establishing clear goals and regularly monitoring progress. Gardening Eden warrants careful attention.

Gardening Principle: Reduce Your Energy Use

Gardening Tip 13: Establish an Energy Budget

Once you have a handle on how much energy you're using, it's time to establish your energy goals. Most of us recognize the wisdom of living within a financial budget. By budgeting, we demonstrate that being prepared for the future is more important than living in the moment. Wise financial stewardship allows us to decrease our long-term dependence on others, achieve goals such as college education for our children, withstand unexpected financial setbacks, and give generously to others.

It is time to treat energy in the same way. Like finances, conventional energy sources are limited and finite. Conserving energy will help our kids and others. Let's use those energy bills we studied previously to establish a realistic budget and goal.

As a component of reducing our carbon footprint, we established a goal to reduce our home energy use. We decided that since our house was fairly new and well insulated, we would try some very simple steps. We lowered our thermostat, replaced some of our standard light bulbs with compact fluorescent bulbs, and paid much more attention to lights left on unnecessarily. Just these simple measures reduced our home energy use by 8 percent between 2006 and 2007. With this success behind us, we are now taking steps to reduce it even more.

Of course, for us to reduce our household energy use by another 10 to 20 percent, we are going to have to be vigilant. Just like balancing our checkbooks, we will need to monitor our energy use carefully and monthly. Then we will be able to make small adjustments to achieve our goal before we get so far "in debt" that we are buried in past-due notices.

Gardening Tip 14: Seal the Envelope

Heating and cooling your house accounts for about 40 percent of the carbon dioxide generated by your home. One of the best first things you can do to reduce your energy use is to make sure that you're getting the most out of the energy you're currently using. Stop the waste. The average house has enough minor and major leaks that the amount of energy wasted equals the energy that would be lost if you kept a small window open year-round. By sealing leaks, adding insulation where it might be missing, and weatherizing doors and windows, you may save a great deal of money that's currently going right out the window, literally. If you live in a warm-weather climate, similar improvements can reduce your air-conditioner load and the cost of keeping your home comfortable. Another benefit: reducing energy use means reducing the amount of carbon dioxide released into the air.

Most local utility companies have home-energy audit and weatherization programs. Often the utility will send a trained professional to your house to evaluate your energy use, search for air leaks and places where you need insulation, and check the efficiency of your heating and cooling equipment.

The U.S. Department of Energy provides a number of resources for utilities and residential customers alike, including detailed information on conducting your own energy audit for your home. You can find these at www.eere.energy.gov/consumer/your_home/energy_audits.

Gardening Tip 15: Plant Trees

The sun can be your friend or foe. It provides warmth in the winter when you want it but also in the summer when you don't. Those bright winter days with the sun low in the sky are wonderful treats and can warm a house in a remarkably short period of time. If you live in the Northern Hemisphere and have windows that face south, take advantage of those windows by planting deciduous trees on the south side of your house. Deciduous trees include maples, oaks, and other trees that lose their leaves in the winter. In summer, the trees will provide dense shade to keep the sun's rays from heating your house, but in the winter, they'll allow the rays to penetrate and warm the house. Think of deciduous trees as creation's self-adjusting curtains.

For many homes in the United States, the summertime sun on the west side of the house is the hardest to deal with. When the sun drops toward the horizon in the late afternoon, it is in the perfect position to bake your west walls and windows. To help prevent this, plant fast-growing trees on the west side of your house. As these trees grow vertically, they will keep your house shaded, protected, and cool.

A landscape architect cannot be expected to leave the subject of trees without waxing a bit philosophical. The Bible is filled with stories of trees and uses them to convey a wide variety of attributes and truths. Trees are the first symbols mentioned in the Bible—the tree of life and the Tree of the Knowledge of Good and Evil (Genesis 2:9). Trees model strength during adversity (Psalm 1:3 and Jeremiah 17:7–8). Trees are resilient (Job 14:7–9). A great tree symbolizes the strength of a great king (Daniel 4:20–22). Just as you can know a tree by its fruit, Jesus said, you can tell true believers from false by their fruit (Matthew 7:17–20). Psalm 52 tell us that God will "uproot" those who turn away from Him, but those who look to the Lord for sustenance flourish like olive trees.

Next to the view of red alders along Fairview Creek that's framed by our living-room window are verses from Scripture, which our friend Margaret Hespen penned in beautiful calligraphy.

> Blessed is the man who trusts in the LORD,
>   whose confidence is in him.
> He will be like a tree planted by the water
>   that sends out its roots by the stream.
> It does not fear when heat comes;
>   its leaves are always green.
> It has no worries in a year of drought
>   and never fails to bear fruit.
>   (Jeremiah 17:7–8)

Oh, that I could be such a tree. As you try to be one…plant one.

Gardening Tip 16: Turn the Thermostat Down

Technological innovations abound in the area of indoor temperature control. Programmable thermostats now make it easy to save tremendous amounts of energy, matching heating and cooling to the times when we need them most. Since about 40 percent of the energy we use in our homes goes to heating and cooling, changes here can make a big difference.

It has been shown that you can save at least 10 percent of your annual energy bills by simply turning your thermostat down ten to fifteen degrees for eight hours during cold weather. A programmable thermostat makes this simple to do this while the house is empty or while everyone is sleeping. Conversely, when it's warm outside, set the thermostat at seventy-eight degrees, and turn it higher when people are sleeping to reduce your nighttime air-conditioner loads.

Keep your thermostat set no higher than sixty-eight degrees when people are up and around in the house during the winter. You'll save about 2 percent of your heating bill for every degree below seventy, so you may want to set your thermostat lower than sixty-eight. When no one is home or everyone is sleeping, lower the setting to fifty-five degrees. Electric blankets or mattress pads are a great alternative to heating the entire house. They deliver the heat to you in a personal and direct way.

Programmable thermostats are not recommended for houses with heat pumps or that rely on electric baseboard heaters. However, since electric baseboard heaters are among the least energy-efficient heating methods, consider changing to a heat pump or central furnace, if possible.

Here's another energy strategy—throw lots of parties. Every guest in your house is the equivalent of a 175-watt space heater. A large group will warm up your house, and you can turn the furnace off! Unless, of course, you are throwing this party in Minneapolis in January. Then I'd advise you keep the furnace on and just turn down the thermostat.

Gardening Tip 17: Change Your Bulbs

Regular light bulbs are known as incandescent bulbs. They haven't changed much since they became widely available in the 1920s. However, they really should be called incandescent "heat" bulbs rather than "light" bulbs because they are terribly inefficient in converting electrical energy into light. As a matter of fact, about 97 percent of the energy going into a regular bulb goes into producing heat, with only 3 percent producing usable light. Regular incandescent bulbs have a lifespan of less than one thousand hours.

In the 1980s, new technology emerged in the development of compact fluorescent lamps (CFLs). These amazing replacements for incandescent bulbs use only about one-fourth the energy and last ten times longer. Replacing just six bulbs in an average house can reduce energy use by more than $32 annually. Since a 100-watt equivalent CFL bulb costs about $1.50, six CFL bulbs could pay for themselves in less than four months. In addition, each bulb you convert from incandescent to CFL will reduce greenhouse gas emissions by about 100 pounds per year.[1]

Many local electrical utilities offer substantial savings on CFLs. There are even giveaways in many communities. Read those fliers that come with your electric bills, and keep your eyes open for an energy fair near you.

Good for creation, good for the pocketbook. Change those bulbs.

Gardening Tip 18: Adjust Your Water Heater

Since more than 10 percent of the energy used in our homes goes to heat water, we need to look at water heaters—the type, size, and settings—to see if there are ways to save energy.

---

1. Richard Heede, "Cool Citizens: Household Solutions," Rocky Mountain Institute, Snowmass, CO, April 2002.

The type of water heater matters because natural gas water heaters are about twice as energy efficient compared with electric water heaters. You can make your water heater more efficient by adjusting the thermostat. People usually set their water-heater thermostats for water temperatures between about 110 and 140 degrees Fahrenheit. Reducing the setting of the thermostat can save energy—about 4 percent for every 10-degree reduction in temperature.

Other things that you can do to increase the energy efficiency of your water heater are to install an insulating blanket, turn the thermostat down or off when you go out of town, and make sure the hot water lines leading out of the tank are insulated. If you need a new water heater, consider one of the new tankless models. They heat water on demand, rather than storing hot water for long periods in a tank, where the water loses heat every minute. There are often state incentives to assist in the purchase of these alternative systems.

Gardening Tip 19: Unplug Chargers

We have become a nation of "phantom power" users. Phantom power is the power used by our dozens of electrical devices when they are turned off. Believe it or not, 75 percent of all the power that is used by our DVD players, computers, televisions, kitchen appliances, and other devices, is used while they are turned off. Cell-phone chargers are even worse—95 percent of their energy is wasted. We're burning needless energy when we're at work, sleeping, or on vacation. Our little electronic leeches continue to suck the juice out of our homes 24/7/365.

So unplug those chargers when you're not using them. Use a power strip with a switch to supply power to your television, stereo, and other devices. Then switch the power strip off when you're not around. You'll save the energy equivalent of leaving a 100-watt incandescent light bulb on continuously.

Gardening Tip 20: Air-Dry Clothes

Your grandmother or great-grandmother had it right—things dry naturally (unless, of course you live in the Pacific Northwest!). But even here, we can save wear and tear on our clothes if we hang them outside on a line, or inside on a rack, to dry. Imagine that—a completely energy-free drying service.

Gardening Tip 21: Look for Energy-Saving Appliances

Appliances use about 20 percent of the annual energy consumed by our homes. Pumps for pools and spas are the thirstiest appliances, closely followed by refrigerators, washing machines, and clothes dryers. Here in the United States, we have several programs in place to help consumers make informed choices about the relative energy efficiency of various appliance makes and models.

If you are looking at a new refrigerator, for example, the required yellow "EnergyGuide" label will tell you two things. First, it will state the estimated annual kilowatt hours of electricity the appliance will use and how it compares to other similar models. Secondly, it will tell you the estimated annual cost to operate that particular fridge.

If a particular model uses 10 to 50 percent less energy or water than standard models, it qualifies for a blue "Energy Star" label. The U.S. Department of Energy even has an online calculator so you can see how much money you could save annually if you replaced your existing refrigerator with an "Energy Star" rated appliance. See www .energystar.gov/index.cfm?fuseaction=refrig.calculator.

Spend a little more up front for efficient appliances, and you can save a significant amount of energy, greenhouse gas emissions, and money.

Gardening Tip 22: Do Remodels Right

Though it is often prohibitively expensive to redo an existing house by putting in new super-efficient wall insulation or new low-emissivity ("Low-E") windows, it is much more possible when constructing something new. The construction industry is innovating rapidly to meet the demands of the marketplace, with new energy-efficient materials and equipment being released almost daily.

184

If you plan to remodel any part of your home, research the newest energy-efficient materials and techniques, and incorporate as many as you can afford in your construction. Studies have shown that it takes only two to six years to pay the extra front-end expense with energy savings. And as energy costs continue to skyrocket, these measures may pay for themselves even sooner.

Gardening Principle: Use Renewable Energy Sources

Gardening Tip 23: Buy Renewable Energy

Wind. Solar. Hydropower. Biomass. Geothermal. Wave action. These and other sources of energy are often called "renewable" or "green." They use existing natural processes to generate energy, and they are renewable when compared with fixed, finite resources such as coal and oil. As the costs of these traditional sources of energy like oil and coal continue to climb, there are increasing incentives for companies to invest in the development of these new technologies.

Many electrical power utilities offer their customers opportunities to choose to have some, if not all, of their power come from renewable sources. Customers pay a bit more, but in return, they lessen the air pollution and carbon-dioxide emissions created by traditional fossil fuel–based power plants. In 2007 Austin Energy led the nation in this arena, selling more than a half a billion kilowatt hours of renewable energy to its customers.

For a national list of "Green Power" programs, visit www.eere .energy.gov/greenpower/markets/pricing.shtml. Sign up and feel better about the energy you do use.

Some of these changes may require spending additional money up front before you see energy savings—changing light bulbs or planting trees, for example. Others, like turning down your thermostat or water heater will result in immediate savings without any up front costs. In either case, perhaps we need to look at energy the way we do cash— we can take steps to avoid spending it, but if we really want to see it increase dramatically, we have to spend money to make money. The key with energy is to try to incorporate both strategies into our daily lives.

11

Transportation in the Garden

The heart of the problem is the internal combustion engine, which has powered America into unparalleled affluence, but now may drive it to unprecedented environmental disaster.

—SENATOR GAYLORD NELSON,
founder of Earth Day

W hat Would Jesus Drive?"

This campaign of the National Association of Evangelicals garnered a great deal of attention when it began in 2002. The campaign pointed out that there is no aspect of our lives that Christ does not want to influence for God's kingdom. Even something as mundane as the car we drive has spiritual implications. As a matter of fact, Christianity becomes irrelevant if it cannot offer moral direction for the unique questions of each time, place, and people. When we assume our responsibilities as gardeners of Eden, we start to think about how all aspects of our lives can best exemplify true stewardship of creation. And almost no area of contemporary culture has a greater impact on the planet than transportation; how we move ourselves around.

Transportation accounts for 28 percent of all energy consumed in the United States. Though there are "green power" choices for our household energy use, virtually all transportation is fueled by oil. Cars, trucks, trains, ships, and planes are all dependent upon petroleum-based fuels. Even hybrid vehicles use oil as their primary energy source, though much more efficiently than conventional cars and trucks. Remember the adage Reduce, Reuse, Recycle? When it comes to transportation, we should modify this to: Reduce, Reduce, Reduce.

Just as when we use less energy in our homes, reducing the amount of energy we use for transportation also offers multiple advantages. The garden becomes less polluted, our pocketbooks are fuller, and our personal health and fitness can improve as we find other ways of moving around. It's hard to argue with the multiple benefits of this three-legged stool:

- environmental benefits
- economic benefits
- health benefits

It's a win-win-win.

190

Gardening Principle: Use Less Fossil Fuel

We are addicted to our cars. We own more of them than ever before, and we drive them more miles than ever before. Consider this: since 1980, the population in the United States has increased by 32 percent, yet the number of miles we each travel in our vehicles has increased at nearly three times that rate.[1] And here's the bottom line: each gallon of gasoline we use in our cars releases 20 pounds of greenhouse gases into the atmosphere. If we are to be effective gardeners, we need to reduce our driving and the pollution it causes. Fortunately, there are many ways we can accomplish this.

Gardening Tip 24: Consolidate Trips

One of the easiest things we can do to save energy is to group our vehicle trips. Rather than drive to the grocery store and home, then to the hardware store and back, and finally out for dinner, turn three trips

---

1. "Latest Findings on National Air Quality: Status and Trends Through 2006," United States Environmental Protection Agency, January 2008.

into one. Most of us do this already, but a little more intentional planning can decrease the amount of fuel we use. Just like holding off running the dishwasher until it is full, saving auto trips until you can accomplish several things at once takes a bit of planning but offers significant savings.

Gardening Tip 25: Walk

In our discussion about food, I pointed out that nearly two-thirds of adults in the United States are obese, which results in all sorts of health problems. Part of the problem is our eating habits, but another contributing factor is our lack of exercise. Most of us lead fairly sedentary lives. If we engage in physical activity, we have to program it into our lives—it doesn't happen naturally the way it did for our grandparents. This sets up the ridiculous situation where people fight for the parking space nearest the entrance to the fitness club.

One of the easiest and most healthy lifestyle changes we can make is to become walkers.

When I was growing up, Sunday dinner was often at my grandparent's house, the one with the "back forty." We would have a barbecue on the back patio and share hamburgers, potato salad, and lots of laughs. After dinner, with few exceptions, the kids and the adults would go for a walk around the San Gabriel neighborhood. We'd walk, talk, chat with neighbors, and just get our metabolisms going again after a big meal. Of course, in those days, no one talked about doing this to achieve fitness goals; we just did it because it felt good.

However, it seems like we've conspired to create communities where walking is actually discouraged. Our homes are far from the nearest grocery store. Wide and intimidating streets are very unfriendly to pedestrians; sidewalks are absent or sporadic; intersections are dangerous to cross.

This is beginning to shift. A new trend in the planning and design of residential developments—called "neo-traditionalism"—results in communities with many of the attributes of older neighborhoods. Houses with front porches set relatively close to the street make it easier to chat with neighbors. Good street lighting, garages accessed by back alleys, and wide sidewalks shaded by trees help re-create the kind of neighborhood that my grandparents lived in. These are some of the characteristics of a walkable community. And the health benefits can be substantial in these communities where cars are accommodated but not allowed to completely dominate the neighborhood.

If you want to know if a street or development meets the requirements of a walkable neighborhood, apply the "Halloween Test." Visit the neighborhood on Halloween night. If you see large numbers of trick-or-treaters, you are most likely in a walkable neighborhood.

In 2005, Vicki and I moved to Fairview Village, a neo-traditional development east of Portland. The first year we lived here, we were warned to be prepared on Halloween. Heeding that advice, we purchased five large bags of candy, enough for a hundred kids or so. We ran out of candy in less than thirty minutes. The continuous parade of princesses, ghouls, and superheroes was completely overwhelming; we had never seen anything like it before. There were no parking places available in the neighborhood that night; the streets were packed with the cars of people who drove their kids here from all over the Portland metropolitan area. The following year, we invited several friends to come over and watch the spectacle with us, and we began to count the little munchkins. In 2006, we ran out of candy and turned out the lights at 7:30, after 350 visitors. In 2007, we decided to move our picnic table to the front porch to better watch the parade. We were able to hang on until about 8:15 and closed it down after 475 trick-or-treaters. In 2008, a clear, cool night encouraged over eight hundred kids to empty our candy bowl! *You* may not be able to recognize a walkable neighborhood, but I guarantee a parent with a six-year-old child can.

Transportation involves movement. Movement requires energy. So each time we need to move, we face a choice—how do I want to "fuel" this movement? I can put gasoline in my car and then burn that gas as the car moves me, with exhaust emanating from the car. Or I can put food in my body and let my metabolism convert that food into energy and allow my body to walk and exhale.

The benefits of walking are numerous. For one, we would all be a lot healthier if we walked, rather than drove, to Starbucks or the grocery store. A brisk, thirty-minute walk five times a week provides a level of activity that the U.S. Surgeon General says will result in greater health and help prevent obesity. In the process, we will burn about 150 calories. On the other hand, if we use the car, that same two mile round trip to the grocery store might burn half a gallon of gas, particularly if the engine is cold.

So if you want to save money, improve your health, and protect creation, become a walker.

Gardening Tip 26: Bike

You never forget how to ride a bike. Or do you? Originally invented as a recreational novelty in the 1800s, bicycles were soon recognized for their great utilitarian function. This amazing human-powered vehicle became a primary means of transportation in many countries.

However, throughout their history, bicycles have been discarded as soon as other motorized transportation machines became available. This continues to be true in much of the developing world. Taipei, Taiwan, was renowned for its use of bikes as the primary means of traversing the city. Taiwan also became one of the biggest bicycle-manufacturing countries in the world, and their bikes were sold domestically and in overseas markets worldwide. However, as the Taiwanese economy boomed and incomes rose, bicycles became more of an export product only. As people became more affluent, they ditched their bicycles in favor of motorized scooters; their two-cycle engines spewing oily, grimy exhaust into the air, turning Taipei's air into some of the most polluted on the planet. Ironically, this bike-producing country became so choked in air pollution that, in 2001, the government offered incentives to encourage residents to use bicycles again.

On the other side of the spectrum, I once visited a city with a population of over a million people where bicycles were the means of transportation for one-third of all trips to work. Let that sink in…one-third of all commuting trips to work made by bicycle instead of by car! And this was not some impoverished, developing country but in Copenhagen, Denmark, a city that in 2008 was ranked eleventh worldwide in a survey of quality of living.[2]

Copenhagen also has a remarkable free bicycle program. Racks all over the city hold special red bicycles. Place a coin in the lock on the bike, and it disengages from the bike rack, making it available for use. You can then ride it all over the city and, when you are done, return it to one of the dozens of similar racks. Insert the locking pin, and out pops your coin deposit. If you're in a rush, just leave the bike anywhere and someone else will likely return it for you in order to pocket the change.

Depending on where you live, what you do for a living, and the facilities at your work, riding a bike may or may not be feasible for you. Some cities, like Portland, have invested extensively in bicycle facilities such as bike lanes, bike paths, and bike parking facilities. Consequently, Portland leads the nation in the number of people who com-

---

2. 2008 Quality of Living Survey, William M. Mercer Consulting, June 2008.

mute by bike at ten thousand per day, or nearly 3 percent of all commuting trips.

Biking to work takes time and some thoughtful preparation. When I commuted to downtown Portland on my bike, fourteen miles each way, I had to stash clothes at the office, take a shower at a nearby gym, and allot a bit more time. This may or not be possible for you. The benefits, however, were well worth the effort. In my ride through the neighborhoods of east Portland, I saw things I never saw from the freeway, I got badly needed exercise, and I achieved a sense of accomplishment. My advice is not to try a cold-turkey switch. Start small— perhaps one day a week—during nice weather, and see if you experience similar benefits. If you do, you'll reduce your global impact by 20 percent, and you'll be healthier and happier for it.

Gardening Tip 27: Drive a More Fuel-Efficient Vehicle

Sure…sometimes we can reduce our driving by consolidating trips, walking, biking, or other means. But sometimes—actually, a lot of times—we must use our cars and trucks to get places. Since our daily lives are filled with a lot of driving, good stewardship practices would encourage us to do so in a way that has the least possible impact. Once again, the less gas we buy, the more dollars stay in our wallets and the less carbon dioxide we make.

Though you might think that the trend in fuel economy has been improving over time, it hasn't exactly panned out that way. Though the fuel economy of individual cars has improved, drivers have developed a preference for bigger, heavier, and less efficient vehicles. In 1987, the average vehicle weighed 3,220 pounds. By 2004, the average vehicle was 26 percent heavier, topping out at over two tons. We fell in love with trucks and SUVs, and we bought them by the millions, replacing our more efficient passenger cars. So, it is not surprising that during that same time period, overall fuel economy declined from 26.2 miles per gallon to 24.6.[3]

I have been driving a hybrid car since 2001. In that time, I have driven about 100,000 miles. Since I have averaged about 42 miles per gallon driving hybrids, I have consumed nearly 2,400 gallons of gasoline. With this gas consumption comes the fact that I am responsible for putting about 48,000 pounds of carbon dioxide into the atmosphere. And that's just the CO_2. It doesn't include the various other types of pollutants that come from the exhaust systems of internal combustion engines. Not something I am very proud of.

Now imagine that instead of driving a hybrid, I had driven a car that achieved average fuel economy, which is generally about 25 miles to the gallon. I would have used 1,600 additional gallons of gasoline (costing me about $6,400 more at today's prices), and dumped another 32,000 pounds of CO_2 into the air you breathe. Quite a difference.

But those are the results using vehicles with *average* fuel economy. If instead, I drove one of the most popular sport utility vehicles such as a Chevy Suburban, Volkswagen Touareg, Jeep Grand Cherokee, Ford Expedition, Toyota Land Cruiser, or Hummer H3, I would have used nearly 6,000 *more* gallons of gasoline (costing $24,000 and creating 120,000 pounds of additional greenhouse gases). That represents over three times the fuel, three times the pollution, and three times the cost of my Prius.[4]

This is not intended to bash particular auto choices. As with every-

---

3. "Revised Summary of Fuel Economy Performance," U.S. Dept. of Transportation and National Highway Traffic Safety Administration, NVS-220, January 15, 2008.

4. If you are interested in comparing the fuel economy of several cars, the U.S. Environmental Protection Agency has an excellent Web site: www.fueleconomy.gov. You can search cars by class, and compare cars side by side to see which are the thirstiest and stingiest cars.

thing else we do, God wants us to count the cost. He wants us to be good stewards of all He has blessed us with. If our daily routine includes transporting a four person ranch crew across an expansive Wyoming ranch to ensure our cattle are well taken care of, perhaps driving a Ford Expedition represents good stewardship. But if we commute on a freeway by ourselves each day, perhaps something a bit more conservative would be a more responsible choice. As with everything else in our lives, He leaves it up to us.

Gardening Tip 28: Live Close to Work

Even better than buying a more fuel-efficient car is driving less. Driving a gas-guzzling SUV twenty miles twice a week is much better than driving a hybrid car forty miles every day. No solution is better than reducing the number of miles you drive. And one way to accomplish this is to work close to where you live.

In 2007 Vicki and I were able to cut the total miles we drove by 50 percent. In addition to consolidating trips, driving a hybrid, and other strategies, one factor made a huge difference—I changed jobs. I was motivated, in part, by a desire to reduce my driving. Instead of commuting nearly thirty miles a day for work, I now drive less than two miles to my workplace at Gresham City Hall. Most days, I now walk to work rather than drive. I'm healthier, and so is the garden.

Living close to where we work, shop, and go to church is often difficult to accomplish, but it has many benefits, not all of which are environmental. We can become more connected in the community where we live. We find that our lives intersect with more people on a broader range of issues. We care more, because we have more at stake. We may even feel prompted to get involved in community activities: volunteering in a neighborhood association or in church activities that help our neediest residents, or even running for a local elected office.

An interesting trend is happening in our nation. From the 1950s to the 1990s, people left cities in droves, fleeing crime, congestion, pollution, and other detritus of urban life. They fled to the suburbs, the idealized place where peace and prosperity were believed to reign supreme. Never mind the effects sprawl had on the garden. With people living farther and farther away from where they worked, we needed to invest billions of dollars in the transportation, water, and other infrastructure arteries that kept the suburbs alive. At the turn of the millennium, nearly half of all households were located in the suburbs.[5] Nearly 80 percent of us were driving alone to work.[6] The pace of our lives continues to quicken unrelentingly, and we rush headlong from here to there, battling traffic, the clock, and skyrocketing fuel prices. And the next generation is reacting.

Many people have decided that suburban life is too detached from the other aspects of community, including places of employment, entertainment, civic life, and houses of faith. They have come to the conclusion that spending two hours each day commuting is a tremendous waste of time as well as energy resources. They have decided to rethink the wisdom of the suburban life.

Where your parents wanted to live is not necessarily where your kids will want to live.

The pendulum has started to swing back toward the urban cores of cities. Smaller household sizes have led young people and empty nesters to share a common desire—a safe, vibrant, culture-filled life in a more urban community. A place where you can walk to a show, to

5. American Housing Survey for the United States: 2005, Figure 3, *Location: 2005*, U.S. Dept. of Housing and Urban Development and U.S. Census Bureau, August 2006.

6. American Housing Survey for the United States: 2005, Table 2-24, Journey to Work—Occupied Units.

the grocery store, and the corner coffee house. A place where a car is only used for weekend excursions to the countryside, mountains, or shore. A place where you don't spend all your spare time mowing the grass or raking leaves. People want to live where they have more time for human interaction, leave more resources for the future, and produce less greenhouse gas emissions.

Deciding to live close to where we work is one way we can better steward creation.

Gardening Tip 29: Use Public Transit

In the summer of 2006, I was invited to participate in an experiment in Portland. It was called "The Low Car Diet." For a solid month I was to try to go without a personal car. Instead, I would walk, bike, use a shared car, and most commonly, use public transit. Living fifteen miles away from my workplace made it a bit challenging, at times. However, our community is well served by light-rail transit, a streetcar line downtown, and a very well-developed bus system. One of the most delightful discoveries was how easily I could combine bike riding and public transit. Both our buses and light-rail trains allow bicyclists to jump aboard after placing their bikes on racks.

The month was successful on two counts. First, I was able to go an entire month without driving my car. Second, and more important, I learned that with a bit of planning, I could go without a car for the vast majority of times I needed to get somewhere else. I found that other options were available that were more beneficial to the environment.

It is difficult to precisely determine how much energy we save by using public transit instead of our own personal vehicles. Variables such as the gas mileage of your personal car, how many people you travel with, and the type and cost of public transit make the calculations very complicated. However, if you live close to public transit and your car gets average or lower fuel economy, you will likely save a substantial amount of energy if you jump on the bus.

Gardening Tip 30: Consider Car-Sharing and Carpooling

The most dramatic way to reduce the amount of energy you and another driver use commuting is to team up. If you and one other person ride together, you cut the energy you both would use individually by half. Carpool with two people, and you have cut it by two-thirds. A full car of four people uses one-fourth the energy the four drivers would use driving separately. No need to change cars, change routes, or change fuels. It's simple, quick, and green.

When oil prices started to rise dramatically in the 1970s, carpooling became quite popular. By 1980, nearly 20 percent of all commute trips involved carpools. However, they have been in a steady decline ever since. Twenty years later, in 2000, about 12 percent of all commuting trips were in carpools. In the same period, the number of people driving alone rose from 64 percent to nearly 76 percent.[7] The hidden price of our independence is increased dependence on foreign oil and greater pollution of our air. Find a co-worker who lives near you and team up.

200

7. Alan Pisarski, *Commuting in America III,* (Washington DC: Transportation Research Board of the National Academies, 2006), 62.

12

At Home in the Garden

The strength of a nation is derived
from the integrity of its homes.

—CONFUCIUS

Our homes probably most accurately reflect our values. They are our places of personal space. Their size and style, what we fill them with, how we decorate them, how we live in them, and how we maintain them tell a great deal about who we really are. We may put on a mask when we are at work or church, but at home, we are the real deal.

And our impacts on the environment begin at home as well. A recent investigation by the Oregonian newspaper arrived at the following conclusion:

> A typical family of three *with* two automobiles living in a 2,000-square-foot house produces 40,000 pounds of carbon dioxide each year.[1]

If we truly want to become gardeners of Eden, then there is no more important place to begin than in our homes. Fortunately, there is no shortage of "Top Ten Lists for a Green Home." Magazines,

---

1. Patrick O'Neill, "Making your breakfast every morning pumps nearly 200 pounds of CO_2 into the air each year. What can you do about it?" *The Oregonian*, November 26, 2006.

television shows, Web sites, and blogs all list tips on how to green up your home. There are even entire books written on ways to live more sustainably at home. The amount of information, however, may seem overwhelming, confusing, and at times, even contradictory. To sort out the primary things that you can do to practice creation care at home, we will focus on four main principles:

- Avoid Stuff
- Make Less Trash
- Be Conservative
- Keep a Healthy House

Gardening Principle: Avoid Stuff

Has any human society ever had the material blessings that we have here in the new millennium? We have been described as a materialistic, consumer society, afflicted with conspicuous consumption. And yet, in spite of our great variety of possessions, we struggle with discontent. Perhaps we are expecting too much from stuff.

The wisest man in the history of mankind, someone who had limitless treasure, provocative harems, fantastic accomplishments, and absolute power wrestled with a similar type of discontent. King Solomon put it this way:

> I denied myself nothing my eyes desired;
> I refused my heart no pleasure....
> Yet when I surveyed all that my hands had done
> and what I had toiled to achieve,
> everything was meaningless, a chasing after the wind.
> (Ecclesiastes 2:10–11)

A man who had it all tells us we shouldn't waste our time trying to find satisfaction in possessions. Yet we don't believe him. So, we continue to pursue, to purchase, to put away. We come perilously close to living as James described the people of his day, "in luxury and self-indulgence" (James 5:5).

Consider the vastness of the commercial enterprises that depend upon making you a consumer of their products or services. They need you to need what they are selling. But their interest in you is very short lived. Once a purchase is consummated, the company shifts its attention to someone who doesn't yet have its product. Virtually no time or attention is given to how to repair, reuse, or dispose of the products you just purchased.

If our cups don't overflow, at least our houses do. Our garages are the storehouses and silos of biblical times; they have become the places where we store up treasures on earth. If this wasn't so, we'd be able to park our cars in them.

Gardening Tip 31: Give Away Your Money

The number one antidote for overconsumption is to rid ourselves of the means. As the apostle Paul said in his encouragement of generosity, "Excel in this grace of giving" (2 Corinthians 8:7). It is tempting to condescendingly agree with this beautiful philosophy, without allowing it to sink in and change us. But Paul's friend Luke doesn't let us off the hook quite so easily. He sets the bar high in this account of how people in the early church supported one another: "Selling their possessions and goods, they gave to anyone as he had need" (Acts 2:45). And Jesus Himself instructed His followers to "Sell your possessions and give to the poor" (Luke 12:33).

We are familiar with this tension in our lives—the desire to *have* battling with the desire to *give.* If we're honest, we can see both desires at play in our lives, and the battle isn't limited to our finances. It swirls around our time, our attention, and other priorities in our lives. God's financial blessings come to us with a stewardship mandate in the same way creation does. They don't belong to us; they're on loan.

Will we take the financial blessings we have received and hoard them or share them? Will we be like the rich fool who builds even bigger barns for all his stuff but fails to demonstrate generosity toward others (see Luke 12:16–20)? Or will we learn that joy, contentment, and happiness are not found in things? If we want our hearts to be full of joy, we have to excel in the grace of giving.

Advent Conspiracy has become an international movement, launched by a local church here in Portland (www.advent conspiracy.org). The mission of the grass-roots campaign is "restoring the scandal of Christmas by worshiping Jesus through compassion, not consumption." AC encourages believers to give rather than consume and to rediscover the supremacy of Christ at Christmas. In 2007, the efforts of the many churches participating in Advent Conspiracy generated over 2.5 million dollars that were channeled to people in need. Excelling in the grace of giving, indeed.

God wants us to be creation stewards who hold tightly to earthly protection and yet hold our earthly possessions loosely. In order to put this into practice, what are you willing to forego or sell? Who will be the recipient of your generosity? No matter what you decide, your generosity will be a spiritual act, benefitting yourself, others, and ultimately creation.

Gardening Tip 32: Rent and Borrow Rather Than Buy

Have you ever noticed the troubles that come with more stuff? The adage describing the two happiest days of a boat owner's life as being the day he buys the boat and the day he sells it rings true for most of us. Material possessions are subject to all the laws of entropy: the car that needs urgent repair, the vacation house that awaits a new roof, the electronic device that awaits a hardware or software upgrade. And yet, we continue to be seduced by the "joys" of ownership.

To combat the urge to possess, consider alternatives to ownership. Take a rototiller, for example. Why should you have this machine taking up space in your garage when you use it once every year to prep the ground for your vegetable garden? Wouldn't it be better stewardship to rent one or borrow one from a neighbor? Similarly, perhaps you can be a lender of some tool or piece of equipment that might come in handy to one of your neighbors.

From friends to libraries to Netflix, there are countless opportunities to obtain things without the tyranny of ownership. The result for the creation is that items are used more often, resulting in a better return on the energy and raw materials that went into manufacturing them and less meaningless stuff made from precious raw materials.

Gardening Principle: Make Less Trash

You and I are trash machines. Each of us generates nearly one ton of waste each year. The 250 million tons of garbage we produce in the United States would fill Giants Stadium at the Meadowlands in New Jersey 737 times each year. That's twice a day, every day.

The environmental consequences of producing so much garbage are staggering. There are the wastes we see—the packaging, garbage, and discarded items that fill our trash cans. Harder to see, however, are the consequential wastes—mining wastes, ash from coal-burning power plants, factory wastes from manufacturing—that are huge invisible components of our domestic waste stream.

In our 250 million tons of annual household waste, nearly half is paper and textiles. Metal, glass, and plastics make up about a quarter of the total. Yard and food waste make up the balance.

Just as we have become much more detached from the production of food in our society, we have similarly become detached from the disposal of waste. Our grandparents recycled things out of necessity; they didn't even need a word to describe this act of conservation. Things are much different in today's world. We live in a disposable society where convenience rules. Garbage is "out of sight, out of mind." We just throw things "away." Do you ever wonder exactly where "away" is? Have you ever been there?

"Away" turns out to be major landfills, transfer stations, and garbage incinerators. Our garbage must be collected, hauled to increasingly remote locations, and disposed of. This is a very energy-intensive process, with its own environmental impacts and a ticking clock. According to a national industry group, several states in the Northeast have less than five years of landfill capacity remaining.[2]

So the less trash we create, the better.

Gardening Tip 33: Minimize Packaging

I needed to replace an ink cartridge in my printer the other day. Once I had the product in hand, I set about to open and install it. I knew the process wouldn't be easy, but I told myself I could overcome.

The first step was to open the clear plastic shell that allowed the product to hang on the rack at the store. As I am sure you are well aware, these hard plastic sarcophagi are not easily penetrated. However, with minor difficulty, my trusty utility knife was able to pierce the

---

2. "MSW Landfills," National Solid Wastes Management Association, http://wastec.is productions.net/webmodules/webarticles/anmviewer.asp?a=463.

transparent shell. I suffered only minor scratches to my hands and wrist—none serious enough to require medical attention—while tearing the shell the rest of the way open.

Step two was to open the colorful, paper-based box upon which was printed a beautiful picture of tropical fish, along with the ink cartridge manufacturer and model number. For an instant, I wondered if I had bought an ink cartridge or supplies for an aquarium. This box was relatively easy to slice with the aforementioned utility knife. As I opened the box, out came the ink cartridge—vacuum packed in a plastic pouch. A pair of scissors made short work of the pouch, and I was finally able to put my hands on the cartridge. After only one more step—removing the plastic sealant tab—I was able to install the cartridge in the printer. Four steps; four layers of packaging. I am sure this is not even close to a record.

Nearly a third of our household waste is made up of packaging. In general, the more processed the item, the more layers of packaging surround it. Amazingly, 9 percent of your grocery bill goes to cover the cost of packaging. Reduce packaging, and stretch your food dollars.

There is also a radical explosion in the technologies associated with packaging. For years, it was fine that ketchup came in a glass bottle— a very simple, easy-to-recycle package. However, squeeze bottles offered to solve a long-standing ketchup crisis—having to thump a full bottle to get the sauce to flow. To accomplish this, and to keep the container airtight—critical for tomato products—manufacturers had to invent an incredibly complicated plastic bottle. So today, a plastic squeeze bottle can consist of six separate layers of plastic, each bonded to another layer with adhesives. Juice boxes that have corresponding layers of cardboard, plastic, Mylar, and metal foil are also very complicated and make recycling extremely difficult.

Even biodegradable packaging is not a panacea. In a typical landfill environment, the bacterial activity that actually breaks down materials happens at a much slower rate than in nature. Even a head of lettuce may persist for years without breaking down because of the lack of exposure to air and sun, which promotes decomposition.

So the bottom line is this: reduce the amount of trash you generate by reducing the amount of packaging you buy. Make packaging one of your purchasing considerations along with price, quality, and locality.

Gardening Tip 34: Avoid Disposables

It started with paper cups. It grew to include milk cartons and paper plates. Then disposable lighters and diapers. Today, almost anything we can imagine is available as a disposable: toothbrushes, syringes, razors, cameras, contact lenses, and just recently, disposable underwear (see www.onederwear.com). Inventor of the disposable cell phone, Randi Altschul, was inspired at a moment when poor reception tempted her to throw her expensive phone out her car window. Realizing that her phone was too valuable to toss, she created a phone that one could hurl if sufficiently motivated.

However, more and more people are realizing that disposable equates with waste. Gardeners of Eden are starting to buck the trend. Disposables are falling out of fashion. Americans are even starting to pick up a very European and Latin American habit—taking their own reusable bags to the grocery store. They take their own insulated mugs into the coffee shop and pass on the paper cups, and they carry personal water bottles rather than buying bottled water. I even know college students who carry around those little insulating sleeves for paper coffee cups and use them over and over again.

What of the big cloth-diaper-versus-disposable-diaper debate? The evidence is fairly compelling: cloth diapers are better for the environment in several ways. They take fewer resources to manufacturer and have a longer life span. The environmental impacts of washing diapers are less than the impacts of making and disposing of disposable diapers. It takes about 200,000 trees and 80,000 pounds of plastic to manufacturer the disposable diapers used in the United States annually. Most of the 19 billion disposable diapers end up in landfills, contributing over 5 million tons of untreated waste to the ground, threatening contamination of surface and ground water. Even those disposables that claim to be biodegradable may persist in landfills for hundreds of years, just like the head of lettuce.

So wherever possible, avoid disposables.

Gardening Tip 35: Don't Buy Bottled Water

America is the envy of much of the world: we have water. One of the major benefits of spending time in a third-world country is the appreciation a person gains for the importance of civilization. While much of the world's poor struggle for a glass of sanitary drinking water, all of the communities in the United States have water systems that deliver fresh, clean water on demand. Almost without exception or disruption, we have access to water at all times.

And yet, we are susceptible to that most American of influences—image. Brands such as Aquafina, Dasani, and Evian promote the health benefits of hydration—using their products, of course. U.S. consumers have taken the bait hook, line, and sinker. Bottled water sales have skyrocketed.

In the past twenty years, we have gone from each drinking about a gallon and a half of bottled water per year to nearly 28 gallons per year—a 1700 percent increase.[3] Do you think we would drink as much bottled

---

3. "Water: H_2O=Life," American Museum of Natural History, November 2007. www .amnh.org/exhibitions/water/?section=fastfacts#.

water if we knew that it is less regulated than tap water, with fewer quality control measures, required tests, and disclosures? The marketers of bottled water have promoted the health benefits of their products without mentioning the quality concerns. Nor do they mention the tremendous environmental price tag that comes with bottled water.

It's not the water that's inside the bottle that has people concerned. After all, it's probably healthier for us to be drinking bottled water than soda pop. Rather, it's the manufacture and transport of the bottles, both before and after being filled, that create such environmental impacts. Manufacturers use 1.5 million barrels of oil to make the petroleum-based plastic bottles we buy in a year.[4] That is enough oil to fuel 100,000 cars for a year. Add the fuel used to transport the water and the fact that three quarters of these bottles end up in landfills, and you can see why some people say that when you buy bottled water, you're actually buying a bottle filled one-fourth with oil. It has become such a significant issue that mayors in such diverse places as San Francisco, Salt Lake City, Minneapolis, and New York have urged their residents to forgo bottled water and drink tap water instead.

There is a huge price tag for consumers as well. A gallon of bottled water costs nearly 2,000 times (that's 200,000 percent) more than a gallon of California tap water provided by the local water authority.[5] In fact, many bottled water companies simply reprocess water from publicly owned municipal systems. So consumers get to pay for their water twice.

So save some pennies and the planet: drink lots of water—from the tap.

4. Tom Paulson, "Thirst for bottled water may hurt environment," *Seattle Post-Intelligencer,* April 19, 2007.

5. Peter H. Gleick, *The World's Water 2004-2005* (Washington DC: Island Press, 2004), 22–23.

Gardening Tip 36: Buy Products in Bulk

Here's another place where environmental and financial stewardship converge. Bulk foods are generally less expensive and have much less packaging. On a recent trip to the store, I compared bulk and prepackaged prices of cashews, sliced almonds, oatmeal, and apple juice. The savings ranged from 19 percent to 68 percent if I bought these items in bulk. And I would save the packaging as well.

For example, if your child needs to take apple juice in her lunch every day, purchase a large container of apple juice and a smaller reusable container. You'll save money and you'll keep those pesky juice boxes out of the landfill.

213

Gardening Tip 37: Recycle

They say you can't teach an old dog new tricks, but I disagree. Americans have learned some new tricks in the last thirty years. Prior to 1980, we recycled less than 10 percent of our trash. However, since 1980, recycling rates have skyrocketed. In 2006, according to the Environmental Protection Agency, we recycled 32.5 percent of our trash. In Portland, we reached a recycling rate of nearly 59 percent, and we've set a goal of 64 percent by 2009.

There are two main reasons recycling is the environmentally responsible thing to do. For one, it is a better way to steward the resources God has given us. Take the mining and production of aluminum, for example.

Aluminum is the world's second-most-used metal, after iron. Aluminum is made from bauxite, an ore that's extracted from large open-pit mines in the earth's crust. The largest bauxite mining area in the world is in western Australia, an area of over two million acres of sensitive jarrah forest, home to a tremendous biological diversity. Because bauxite occurs near the surface, these lands are stripped of trees and topsoil, down to an impervious clay layer. The soil is then processed and the bauxite removed. Though there have been some recent restoration success stories in Australia, most open pit mines around the world remain scars on the earth indefinitely.

In addition to the impacts of clear-cutting and mining, the production of aluminum from bauxite requires enormous amounts of electricity. In fact, approximately 3 percent of all energy used on the planet goes to produce aluminum. On the other hand, recycling aluminum requires only 5 to 10 percent of the energy used in producing new aluminum from ore. So recycling saves both valuable habitat and energy. Given a choice between buying beverages in either plastic bottles or aluminum cans, choose the cans—they will most certainly be recycled.

The second reason to recycle is that it minimizes the impact of landfills and garbage incinerators on the environment. Keep things out of landfills and you reduce the size and extent of the landfills.

You may have curbside pickup of recyclable material, which makes recycling easy. However, you may live in a community where recycling takes considerably more effort. You may have to sort your glass, paper, plastic, and metals into separate piles and then take them somewhere for recycling. A Web site called Earth 911 at www.earth911.org offers an easy way to find your recycling options. It allows you to enter your location and what you want to recycle, and then it tells you your nearby options.

If your community does not have an active recycling program, consider talking to your elected representatives about establishing one. When Pastor Tri Robinson of Boise Vineyard Church in Idaho tried to offer his church parking lot as a community recycling center, he found that the city of Boise did not have an adequate system in place. Pastor Robinson and his congregation were able to prompt the city to expand its recycling efforts and, in the process, make the community greener.

Gardening Tip 38: Reduce Junk Mail

103,500,000,000. That's the number of pieces of junk mail sent to U.S. households in 2007—over 100 billion. That's nearly 350 pieces for every man, woman, and child in the country. If you feel like you're drowning in a flood of junk mail, you're not alone.

Though mostly unwanted, these free mailings cost the environment dearly. Nearly 100 billion gallons of water and 100 million trees go into creating the printed pieces. And these numbers don't even include the environmental impact of transporting these mailings in trucks, cargo planes, and postal vehicles. Or to take them from your house to the landfill.

Most of these junk mailings go for naught—97 percent is ignored. Trees, water, and fuel are sacrificed for no apparent effect. The Environmental Protection Agency estimates that 4 million tons of junk mail go straight to landfills, unopened. Only about one-fourth of all junk mail is recycled.[6]

Catalogs are the worst offenders. Though they comprise only 15 percent of the total number of junk mailings, they account for the majority of the weight and bulk. Last November, we set a record for one day when we received seventeen catalogs in our mailbox!

Thankfully, there are now several ways to stop the madness. An Internet search will find several organizations that will reduce the amount of junk mail you receive, for a fee. GreenDimes (www.greendimes.com) will contact a dozen direct mail groups and request that your name be removed. In addition, their Web site allows you to continually update your preferences, including listing individual catalogs that you want to stop receiving. Another similar service is 41Pounds

6. Liz Galst, "Stop junk mail for good," Salon.com, December 17, 2007, www.salon.com/mwt/good_life/2007/12/17/junk_mail/.

(www.41pounds.org), named for the average amount of junk mail a person receives in a year. The company also donates $15 of your $41 fee to your choice of several nonprofits dedicated to environmental protection.

Even the direct-mail industry is noticing consumer frustration. According to the Direct Marketing Association, starting in October 2008, every single piece of junk mail will contain information describing the steps you can take to be removed from the company's mailing list. The DMA also offers an online registration process to reduce your junk mail at www.dmachoice.org/consumerassistance.php.

A similar government program is available to remove your name from telemarketing lists so that you don't receive unwelcome phone calls (www.donotcall.gov).

Gardening Tip 39: Compost

In many communities, food and yard waste go to the same place everything else goes—into the trash can and then to the landfill. But in a growing number of communities, organic wastes like these are put in separate bins and go to an entirely different destination—a composting facility. Though this is a positive development, there is an even better option. Don't haul it off in the first place.

If you live in a house that has a yard, it's very easy to keep your grass, leaves, and other yard debris out of the waste stream—compost them yourself. A simple plastic bin in your yard will help you convert these "wastes" to something valuable; a dark, nutrient-rich humus. This "black gold" can be worked back into your yard or garden soil to make the soil more productive the next season. Think of it as your own personal recycling center.

Of course, composting is not a new invention. Farmers have been composting manure and organic material for thousands of years, since long before industrial fertilizers became easily accessible. This gentle way of reintroducing nutrients and organic material does not bring the same risks that many industrial fertilizers bring. It also requires no additional energy.

To the amusement of our kids and friends, Vicki and I recently got some new pets to help with our composting effort. Our new "Worm Factory" uses red worms to convert our kitchen food scraps and shredded paper into worm castings, a great soil additive. Although they aren't very cuddly, these guys work hard at converting waste into a resource. Best of all, they came with a great environmental bumper sticker: "Promote Global Worming."

Gardening Tip 40: Don't Toss It; Gift It

Are you ever amazed by what some people will buy? There is virtually nothing you have that someone else doesn't want or would be willing to pay for. The garage sale of your parent's day has morphed into selling on eBay or Craigslist, trading on exchange sites, or giving things away at Freecycle.org. So rather than throw something out in the trash, sell it, and do something meaningful with the money.

Gardening Principle: Be Conservative

As gardeners of Eden, we want to fulfill our calling in all areas of our lives by using resources more efficiently and effectively. We realize that waste is not good stewardship, so we use less energy at home, drive less to reduce fuel consumption, and create less trash. These are all ways that we become more conservative. We strive to be liberal in love, conservative with resources.

Gardening Tip 41: Use Low-Flow Toilets and Shower Heads

Over half of our water use occurs in our bathrooms. Toilets alone account for one-third of our indoor water consumption. Toilets manufactured after 1992 are required to use no more than 1.6 gallons per flush. Older toilets use anywhere from three to seven gallons per flush. So one of the first things to do is to replace any outdated toilets. Keep your eyes open for the new dual-flush toilets that are coming into the residential market. They allow you to choose the quantity of the flush you need: .8 gallons or 1.6 gallons.

Shower heads are next. Your old shower head may use more than six gallons per minute, but it can be easily replaced with one that uses one-third as much water—two gallons per minute. These low-flow shower heads inject air with the water so you do not have to give up water pressure when you replace the old shower head.

These two changes alone could reduce your bathroom water use by three-fourths. And in an era where there is plenty of talk about droughts and water shortages, this could be good for both the planet and your pocketbook.

Gardening Tip 42: Take Shorter Showers

Many places in the United States are experiencing severe drought conditions. Reservoirs are at their lowest levels in years, and there are incentives to conserve water. Even if you aren't living in an area where water rationing is imminent, it pays to conserve both water and energy. One place these two resources intersect is in the shower. Many of us use our morning showers to move us from comatose to coherent, not from dirty to clean.

According to the EPA, showering is responsible for 17 percent of indoor water use. A typical shower uses six to eight gallons of water a minute. If your daily showers match the U.S. average of ten minutes each day, this means that you use 22,000 to 30,000 gallons of heated water each year. By reducing your shower time to a recommended five minutes, you could be conserving up to 15,000 gallons of water each year.

Another way to accomplish the same thing is to take "navy showers." On a ship surrounded by salt water, fresh water is at a premium. When I was a sailor, we were required to get wet and then immediately shut off the water. Soap up without water flowing, then turn the water back on and rinse. Many low-flow shower heads incorporate a button or lever to accomplish the same thing without having to fuss with the faucets.

219

To keep your shower time down to five minutes, get yourself a timer, or give yourself the time it takes to play one song on your shower radio. (Just make sure the song isn't Springsteen's "Jungleland," which is more than nine minutes long.)

Gardening Tip 43: Go Digital

Our new wired homes allow us to accomplish many new things remotely, instantly, and digitally. We used to have to receive paper bills in the mail, open them, discard the dozen offers for a "diamond-look" bracelet, fill out a paper payment stub, write a paper check, enclose them all in an envelope and affix postage, and send again through the mail. No longer. We can now pay bills online, or have them automatically deducted from our accounts. Saves paper, saves time, saves money.

Likewise, we used to need paper copies of everything. Now, however, we can read, edit, respond, forward, and file documents electronically, all without ever printing hard copies. This saves us nearly a cent a page when you include the cost of paper, ink, and energy. The savings to the environment are significant as well.

Gardening Tip 44: Use Environmentally Friendly Landscaping
We Americans love our lawns. For over a century, the well-manicured lawn has been the ideal of residential landscapes. However, as most homeowners know, maintaining this ideal-looking lawn is neither easy nor natural.

First, there is the watering. Lawns require about one inch of water per week. Assuming a growing season and irrigation period of about twenty-four weeks, you'll need to apply about 15,000 gallons of water for every thousand square feet of lawn each year.

Then there are the chemical cocktails we pour on the grass: fertilizers to keep the grass green, herbicides to kill weeds, pesticides to kill grubs and bugs, fungicides to kill mushrooms. According to a recent estimate, Americans use seventy million pounds of pesticides to maintain our lawns. We're just now discovering the effects of these chemicals on human health.

"Every day of every week, we are continuing in this country to expose children to chemicals whose toxicity is simply not known," said Dr. Philip Landrigan, a world-renowned pediatrician and epidemiologist, and director of the Children's Environmental Health Center at Mount Sinai School of Medicine in New York. "As a pediatrician, I urge parents to think carefully about the choices they make, especially about pesticides.... Pesticides are used in enormous amounts in homes, schools and day care centers and on lawns and gardens. Once released, they are immediately widespread in the environment and create enormous potential for harmful health effects."[7] Lawns are costly financially, environmentally, and to our health.

Lawns are ideal in areas where we need a walkable outdoor surface to

---

7. J.B., Interview with Dr. Philip Landrigan, *E: The Environmental Magazine*, September 2001.

play on. However, we plant lawns everywhere, simply for their aesthetic appeal. There are more environmentally friendly alternatives. Native plants, drought tolerant plants, and plants that attract butterflies, hummingbirds, and other wildlife are alternative design strategies that provide both aesthetic and ecological benefits. There are also many biological and nontoxic alternatives to pesticides and chemical fertilizers. These include ladybugs for aphid control, soaps for insect control, and organic fertilizers. Bird feeders, birdbaths, and hummingbird feeders are other strategies that can work with landscaping to turn your yard into Eden.

Gardening Tip 45: Use Automatic Sprinkler Systems

For lawns and other home landscaped areas, applying water frugally and effectively is important. The best way to do this is to invest in a highly efficient, automatic sprinkler system. A professional with a thorough knowledge of your climate, soils, and local plants should design the system. To the greatest extent possible, try to minimize the amount of spray irrigation, replacing it with high-efficiency drip systems. These systems apply water directly to the roots of individual plants and avoid losing water to the foliage, ground, and air as conventional spray systems do.

Two other elements are key to your irrigation system. Ensure that your programmable irrigation controller has a rain sensor that can easily place it into a hold mode. This will prevent the ridiculous sight of sprinklers operating during a rainstorm. Secondly, sprinkler systems need to be periodically adjusted and monitored to ensure that the water is getting to the plants that need it, instead of the pavement around them.

Gardening Tip 46: Become a Consumer of Recycled Materials

If you are going to recycle your glass, plastic, paper, and metal, you want to make sure that you are a consumer of recycled products as well. But what do the various terms in the marketplace really mean?

- *Recycled content* means that the product is made from materials that normally would have been discarded into the waste stream. The material could come from products that are recovered during initial manufacturing (preconsumer) or after consumer use (postconsumer). If the product does not consist entirely of recycled content, it must be labeled with the percentage of recycled content.

- *Postconsumer content* refers to materials that have been used once and then have been reconstituted to create the new product. Paper, aluminum cans, and carpeting made from recycled plastic milk jugs are examples.

- *Recyclable* means that these products can be easily collected and remanufactured into new products after their current life.

- *Biodegradable* or *degradable* are used to describe products that will break down naturally if exposed to the proper amount of air, light, and water. Unfortunately, this label is relatively meaningless, since most landfills prevent normal biological degradation due to facility design.

A comprehensive guide to understanding claims made on labels is maintained by Consumer Reports. Access it at www.greenerchoices.org/ecolabels.

There are nearly five thousand recycled-content products available in the United States. A comprehensive directory of products is maintained by the state of California at www.ciwmb.ca.gov/RCP. For a directory of products made from recycled plastics, go to www.american chemistry.com/s_plastics/sec_rppd.asp.

Reduce your contribution to the waste stream by buying recycled.

Gardening Principle: Keep a Healthy House

So we've changed our food habits and reduced our energy use, we drive our cars less, and we've taken steps to accumulate less stuff and produce less trash. But at the end of the day, we come home to our house, apartment, condominium, or mobile home. Home Sweet Home may be no such thing. Recent scares about radon levels, plastics, and water contaminated by pharmaceuticals have us concerned. What are some steps to make sure that our homes do not contribute to the polluting of the garden?

Gardening Tip 47: Avoid Toxic Materials

Toxic chemicals are all around us. The problem is that by the time we notice them, our health may have been robbed.

Radon is a naturally occurring radioactive gas that is known to cause lung cancer in humans. It is generated from the decay of uranium in soils around our homes. It enters homes through cracks in concrete foundations and walls, gaps around utility pipes, and through other openings in the building envelope. The EPA estimates that one out of fifteen homes in the United States has radon levels high enough for concern. Some areas of the country are more susceptible than others. The first step is to purchase an easy-to-administer radon test kit or hire a professional to conduct the test. For more information, see the EPA Web site at www.epa.gov/radon.

Recently scientists have become concerned about the clear polycarbonate water bottle, which has long been thought of as an eco-friendly, refillable alternative to bottled water. However, recent studies have shown that these bottles (usually identified by a number 7 inside the three chasing arrows recycling symbol) can leach the chemical bisphenol-A (BPA), which can disrupt hormones in humans. It is of serious concern for pregnant mothers. The bottles are more likely to leach these chemicals when heated. The polycarbonate water bottle now joins polyvinyl chloride (PVC) plastic and polystyrene on the list of plastics that can leach hormone disruptors and carcinogens. Better living through plastics, indeed.

Other common toxins in our homes include paints, yard and garden chemicals, rat and mouse poisons, drain cleaners, fuel for barbecues, cleaning supplies, fluorescent light bulbs, rechargeable batteries, mothballs, and even some common household plastics. Improper or extended exposure to these and other common household items can cause health problems in our homes, as well as environmental concern when they are disposed of elsewhere.

Gardeners of Eden will bring fewer of these toxins into their homes and dispose of the ones they have safely.

Gardening Tip 48: Use Healthy Cleaning Supplies

I picked up a common household bathroom cleaner the other day and read this warning:

> HAZARD TO HUMANS AND DOMESTIC ANIMALS. CAUSES
> EYE IRRITATION. DO NOT GET IN EYES OR SKIN OR ON
> CLOTHING. WASH THOROUGHLY WITH SOAP AND WATER
> AFTER HANDLING.

The warnings go on to say that if you get any of this miracle cleaner in your eyes, you should rinse for fifteen to twenty minutes (that sure seems like a very long time...) and call a poison control center or doctor for advice. Can this really be a good thing to have in our homes or in the garden?

Most of the toxins in our homes are there because we brought them intentionally. Cleaning supplies are the biggest source of these toxic chemicals. Though most of us use these products with no apparent adverse health effects, the cumulative effects of exposure to a wide variety of chemicals in our environment are unknown. Common ingredients including ammonia, chlorine bleach, and a variety of chemical solvents can pose health problems for some people in certain conditions. In addition, these toxins are not stationary, but mobile—after leaving your house, they move down the waste stream—ending up somewhere else in the garden.

An alternative is to use nontoxic cleaning supplies. Using common household ingredients such as vinegar, lemon juice, linseed oil, baking soda, borax, and salt, you can keep your house clean without the toxic chemicals. The state of Vermont has a handy brochure on safe cleaning alternatives at www.cvswmd.org/pdf/non-toxic_cleaners.pdf.

A national spokesperson for removing toxins from our homes is Debra Lynn Dadd. She is the creator of Debra's List at (www.debras list.com), which is a clearinghouse of information on healthy alternatives to toxins. In her book *Home Safe Home,* Debra assures us:

> Don't expect to change your whole house overnight; the very nature of change is a gradual process.... Deciding to make the changes is the hardest part. Finding safe products is easy and can be fun, and you'll love the simplicity of the safe alternatives you can make at home.[8]

Our health, our family's health, and the garden will all benefit from these changes.

---

8. Debra Lynn Dadd, *Home Safe Home,* (New York: Penguin Putnam, 1997).

Gardening Tip 49: Keep Air Filters Clean

Most of our homes rely on a mechanical, forced-air system to move air around. In the summer, the air is air-conditioned, and in the winter it is heated. All of these systems contain a filter to remove dust, pet dander, and other sources of indoor air pollution. To help improve our indoor air quality, we need to regularly clean or replace the filters. It is common for these filters to be one-inch thick and made from fiberglass and paper. These are not very effective, removing only about 10 percent of the small particles in the air, and should be replaced several times each year. In addition, they are disposable, resulting in waste that ends up in a local landfill.

A more effective filter, both for your air quality and the environment, is a permanent, washable filter. High-efficiency filters can remove 60 to 95 percent of household airborne pollution, and both disposable and washable high-efficiency filters are available. Install a washable filter, and breathe a lot easier.

Gardening Tip 50: Use Water Filters

In October 1998 an investigative report in *USA Today* asked, "How Safe is Your Water?"[9] According to the report, millions of Americans have water coming through their home faucets that exceed legal limits for a variety of hazardous contaminants. Ten years later, in March 2008, an investigation by the Associated Press turned up the presence of pharmaceuticals in the drinking water of more than 40 million Americans.[10] Chlorine, added to many municipal water systems, makes these drugs even more toxic.

The contamination of our water supply has health implications for

---

9. Peter Eisler, Barbara Hansen, and Aaron Davis, "Drinking Water's Hidden Dangers," *USA Today*, October 21, 1998.

10. Jeff Donn, Martha Mendoza, and Justin Pritchard, "Drugs Found in Drinking Water," *USA Today*, March 10, 2008.

all of God's creatures. It's alarming that many of these same chemicals have been detected in surface streams and deep aquifers in addition to municipal water supplies.

To help prevent further contamination, never flush unused pharmaceuticals down the toilet or drain. Take them to a nearby clinic or hospital for proper disposal.

Also, consider installing a home-wide water filtration system. Most of these systems contain a carbon filter cartridge that can remove chlorine, organic chemicals, pesticides, and herbicides, while improving the taste of water. A system that also includes reverse-osmosis increases the chances of removing many pharmaceuticals as well.

More information is available from the Environmental Protection Agency at www.epa.gov/OGWDW/faq/faq.html or the Water Quality Association, an international trade organization, at www.wqa.org.

• • •

There you have it—fifty ways to live in a home that is healthier, saves money, and keeps the garden green. No one can expect to put all of these changes into place all at once. Start with the "low hanging fruit," and make small steps toward becoming a gardener of Eden. This is what Vicki and I have done.

Over the past couple of years, we have tried various steps. Some worked, and others we abandoned, all the while growing in our ability and understanding. We have been motivated by dozens of people who have shown us how. We also have had the opportunity to serve as a source of amusement for more than a few family and friends! The process of experimentation has been intellectually challenging, spiritually fulfilling, and actually quite fun. As a result, we have grown to appreciate the creation and love the Creator even more.

13

Cultivating a Life as a Gardener

How can you love your neighbor if you
don't know how to build or mend a fence,
how to keep your filth out of his water supply
and your poison out of his air?… How can you be
a neighbor without *applying* principle—without
bringing virtue to a practical issue? How will
you practice virtue without skill?

—WENDELL BERRY, *The Gift of Good Land*

W hy should I worry about recycling my water bottle?" the University of Oregon coed asked after my talk. "I mean, even if I recycle my one bottle, it isn't going to make any difference to the overall state of the environment."

She had stumbled upon one of the great conundrums of creation care. With nearly 6.7 billion people on the planet, and 304 million in the United States, what difference does my little insignificant life make on a global scale? I can't stop global warming, even if I do give up my SUV. I can't halt the razing of tropical rain forests, even if I don't buy Brazilian soybeans or beef. I can't prevent oil spills in Alaska, even if I do walk more and drive less.

So why bother trying?

Life is filled with rhythms. Rhythms of sunrise and sunset, lunar cycles, and seasons. In the Old Testament, God established rhythms for man and land. Every seventh day was ordained to be a day of rest for men and women. God understood us pretty well; He knew that there would be six days of intense activity that would sap our strength. We would need the seventh day to rest and recharge our batteries.

The land, too, was in danger of being overworked. The Jews were told that when they reached the Promised Land, they could sow fields and harvest crops for six years, but then there should be a Sabbath year. The land needed rest to remain healthy. He even set forth rules about the value of land in real estate transactions, reminding the Jews that "the land is mine and you are but aliens and my tenants" (Leviticus 25:23).

This Sabbath year was also meant to accomplish something beyond helping the land to refresh and man to recharge. The Sabbath year also was a time to cancel debts and wipe the financial slate clean between people. After forgiving debts, God's people were instructed to make one more sacrifice: "There will always be poor people in the land. Therefore I command you to be openhanded toward your brothers and toward the poor and needy in your land" (Deuteronomy 15:11).

The Jews were not asked to solve poverty or end homelessness. In fact, it is clear from this verse and from Jesus's teachings on the same subject that this is not possible; we will always be confronted with poverty. God's point was not the solution, but rather the act. God wants my priorities to align with His, and the way He can tell if they do is by what I do—my actions. Will I follow His direction and help the poor? Not the corporate "we," but the individual "me"; will I do it?

God is not asking you as gardeners to solve global climate change, to end pollution, to stop species extinction. He is just asking you to hold your lives and resources in open hands and to let go when asked. Will you do it?

So, back to the young woman's question. Yes, we should recycle the water bottle because it is 1) a good thing to do, 2) within our power to do, and 3) a small act of worship from us to the Creator. No act, no matter how small, goes unnoticed or is without worth in the spiritual economy.

God tells me that His creation is precious to Him. Therefore, I am to carefully consider how I live: my decisions, my habits, and my impact in the garden. I must not worship either the creation's beauty or mankind's brilliance; I am to reserve my worship for the One who created me. I must be careful that I treat my fellow travelers with the kind of love due daughters and sons of the Most High. Likewise, I am to tread lightly on the Earth, knowing that it is not mine to trash; I am but an alien or tenant.

This brings us back to the vexing question: How green is green enough? Is light green okay, or do I need to be dark green? In other words, do I have to become a vegan pedestrian nudist? Must I sell my car, grow hemp, and live off the land to be a true gardener of Eden?

I can't say what you should do. Though we are fellow travelers, your journey is different. Vicki and I don't even have all the answers, green or otherwise, for our journey. In fact, I seek guidance on a whole host of life's persistent questions:

How much money should I give away?

How much mercy should I show others?

How much of "my" time should I give up?

How many times do I need to turn my cheek, bite my tongue, and keep from smacking that fool silly?

These queries serve as our ongoing dialogue with our Creator. He wants us to wrestle with them; to struggle consciously with our proper response; to come to Him for guidance, direction, and hope. In fact, if we are not wrestling with these questions, our spiritual life is probably floundering on the rocks, not under sail.

Jesus addressed this in an enigmatic parable, encouraging us to be alert and always ready for His return: "From everyone who has been given much, much will be demanded; and from the one who has been entrusted with much, much more will be asked" (Luke 12:48).

But He leaves us asking, "How much is much? How green is green enough?"

Vicki and I have not yet arrived at this answer. We've established goals to reduce our environmental footprint but have not achieved all of them yet. A week does not go by that we don't learn of a new gardening idea worthy of consideration. Some of them we try to hang on to; others we let go of.

We have loved driving a hybrid since our first one arrived in 2001. We have tried several alternative laundry soaps, with no success. Our compost bin has become a destination for our neighbors, giving us more opportunities to interact. Yet, sometimes I buy food that came from foreign countries. And the jury's still out on the composting worms.

But the point is not what we've done or haven't done, anyway. The point is whether we're making progress and whether we continue to be open to change. Am I really committed to a better way of living that's more respectful of the planet? Am I willing to keep the dialogue open with the Creator so that He can reveal His expectations and opportunities to me? Am I willing to change the coffee I buy so that Felipe Castro can send his kids to school? Am I willing to reduce the amount of water and chemicals my yard requires? Am I willing to turn my thermostat down?

This book has not been about telling you what you should do, any more than it is about pointing a finger at the big, bad oil companies. The ultimate battle we all face is with ourselves, not others. After all of the rhetorical chaff is blown away, laid bare is one issue: your willingness to give up what you want. For the sake of the creation, for the sake of your fellow humans, for the sake of the Creator. Are you and I willing to make sacrifices for them?

John Stott, the renowned British Bible scholar and one of *Time Magazine's* top 100 heroes and icons in 2005, focuses a laser beam on the problem—us:

We must learn to think and act ecologically. We repent of extravagance, pollution and wanton destruction. We recognize that human beings find it easier to subdue the earth than they do to subdue themselves.[1]

Though I have long considered myself an environmentalist, the transfer of responsibility from the global "we" to "me" has come more intensely in recent years. I acknowledge the struggle to subdue my own selfish desires. I feel like I have a lot more to learn and a lot more to sacrifice before I am the gardener that my Lord would like me to be. Thankfully, He is gentle with me, and my journey is not yet over.

Each day, the Creator places me back in the garden afresh. *I'd like you to tend and care for this planet,* He whispers. *If you do, the creation will thrive, your fellow brothers and sisters will benefit, and I will be pleased. It's a dirty job, but you will never regret a single day when you're gardening Eden.*

235

---

1. John Stott, *Issues Facing Christians Today* (Grand Rapids, MI: Zondervan, 2006).

Resources

Food

Organizations	
CHEFS COLLABORATIVE http://chefscollaborative.org	According to the Web site, "Chefs Collaborative works with chefs and the greater food community to celebrate local foods and foster a more sustainable food supply."
FARMERS' MARKETS www.farmersmarket.com	Provides a directory of farmers' markets by state
LOCAL HARVEST www.localharvest.org/csa	Offers a directory of farmers' markets, community supported agriculture (CSAs), organic farms, grocery co-ops
SLOW FOOD USA www.slowfoodusa.org	According to the Web site, Slow Food is a global, grass-roots movement that links the pleasure of food with a commitment to community and the environment. The Web site provides information on programs, local chapters, and more.

Books	
Dominion Scully, Matthew	St. Martin's Press, New York, NY, 2002
Food & Faith Schut, Michael	Living the Good News, Denver, CO, 2006
Slow Food: The Case for Taste Petrini, Carlo	Chelsea Green Publishing, White River Junction, VT, 2001
The Gift of Good Land Berry, Wendell	North Point Press, New York, NY, 1981
The Omnivore's Dilemma Pollan, Michael	The Penguin Press, New York, NY, 2006
What Are People For? Berry, Wendell	North Point Press, New York, NY, 1990

Articles

"Buy Local Produce and Save the World"
Conner, Steve, *The Independent,* March 3, 2005.
www.independent.co.uk

"Excess Deaths Associated with Underweight, Overweight, and Obesity"
Flegal, Graubard, Williamson, & Gail, *The Journal of the American Medical Association* 293, no. 15, April 20, 2005.
http://jama.ama-assn.org/cgi/content/full/293/15/1861

Articles continued

"Farmers' Markets Go Beyond Green"

Moskin, Julia, *The New York Times,* May 24, 2006.

www.nytimes.com/2006/05/24/dining/24mark.html

"Food Study Reveals Hidden £9bn Costs of Transport"

Lawrence, Felicity, *The Guardian,* July 15, 2005.

www.guardian.co.uk/news/2005/jul/15/food.greenpolitics

"Global Trade = Global Warming"

Venkat, Kumar, Common Dreams.org News Center,

December 11, 2003.

www.commondreams.org/views03/1211-02.htm

"Health Benefits of Organic Food"

Heaton, Shane, *Grinning Planet,* Issue 149.

www.grinningplanet.com/2005/12-27/health-benefits-of-organic-
food-article.htm

"Imported Food Rarely Inspected"

Bridges, Andrew, Associated Press, *USA Today,* April 16, 2007.

www.usatoday.com/news/nation/2007-04-16-imported-food
_N.htm

"Shopper's Guide to Pesticides in Produce," 5th Edition

Environmental Working Group

www.foodnews.org

Articles continued

"The Practical Guide: Identification, Evaluation, and Treatment of Overweight and Obesity in Adults"

National Heart, Lung and Blood Institute

www.nhlbi.nih.gov/guidelines/obesity/practgde.htm

"U.S. Per Capita Food Supply Trends: More Calories, Refined Carbohydrates, and Fats"

USDA Economic Research Service 25, no. 3

www.nhlbi.nih.gov/guidelines/obesity/practgde.htm, 2002

Web Sites

USDA ALTERNATIVE FARMING SYSTEMS INFORMATION CENTER http://afsic.nal.usda.gov	Information on community supported agriculture, sustainable agriculture, organic production, and more
USDA FOOD AND NUTRITION INFORMATION CENTER http://fnic.nal.usda.gov	Information on food labeling, food safety, nutrition, and childhood obesity

Energy

Organizations

ARBOR DAY FOUNDATION www.arborday.org	Nation's largest organization promoting the planting and caring for trees. Lots of information about trees.

Organizations continued

ENERGY INFORMATION ADMINISTRATION www.eia.doe.gov	Official energy statistics from the U.S. government
U.S. DEPARTMENT OF ENERGY: ENERGY EFFICIENCY AND RENEWABLE ENERGY www.eere.energy.gov	A clearinghouse of information on energy efficiency for consumers

Articles

"Cool Citizens: Household Solutions" Rocky Mountain Institute
www.rmi.org/images/other/Climate/C02-12_CoolCitizensBrief.pdf

"Landscaping for Energy Efficiency"
National Renewable Energy Laboratory
www.nrel.gov/docs/legosti/old/16632.pdf

Web Sites

ENERGY STAR APPLIANCES
www.energystar.gov/index.cfm?c=appliances.pr_appliances

ENERGY STAR PROGRAM
www.energystar.gov

U.S. DEPARTMENT OF ENERGY: ENERGY EFFICIENCY AND
RENEWABLE ENERGY: GREEN POWER NETWORK
www.eere.energy.gov/greenpower/markets/pricing.shtml

Web Sites continued

NATURAL RESOURCES DEFENSE COUNCIL: GREEN ADVISOR: APPLIANCES, ELECTRONICS, AND HVAC

www.nrdc.org/enterprise/greeningadvisor/pu-appliances.asp

THE NATURE CONSERVANCY: CARBON FOOTPRINT CALCULATOR

www.nature.org/initiatives/climatechange/calculator

242

THE CLIMATE TRUST CARBON CALCULATOR

www.carboncounter.org

One of the best carbon footprint calculators

U.S. DEPARTMENT OF ENERGY: HOME ENERGY AUDITS

www.eere.energy.gov/consumer/your_home/energy_audits/

U.S. DEPARTMENT OF ENERGY: LANDSCAPING

www.eere.energy.gov/consumer/your_home/landscaping/index.cfm

U.S. ENVIRONMENTAL PROTECTION AGENCY: PERSONAL EMISSIONS CALCULATOR

www.epa.gov/climatechange/emissions/ind_calculator.html

Transportation

Organizations

NATIONAL HIGHWAY TRAFFIC SAFETY ADMINISTRATION www.nhtsa.gov	Information on vehicles, fuel economy, commuting, and vehicle safety

Books	
Commuting in America III Pisarski, Alan	Transportation Research Board, Washington DC, 2006

Articles

"American Housing Survey for the United States: 2005"
U.S. Department of Housing and Urban Development and U.S.
Department of Commerce
www.census.gov/prod/2006pubs/h150-05.pdf

"Automotive Fuel Economy Program: Annual Update Calendar Year 2003"
National Highway Traffic Safety Administration
www.nhtsa.gov/cars/rules/CAFE/FuelEconUpdates/2003/index.htm

"What Would Jesus Drive?" Discussion Paper
Ron Sider and Jim Ball
www.whatwouldjesusdrive.org/resources/wwjdrive_paper.pdf

"Latest Findings on National Air Quality: Status and Trends Through 2006"
U.S. Environmental Protection Agency
www.epa.gov/airtrends/2007/index.html

Web Sites

U.S. DEPARTMENT OF ENERGY: AUTOMOBILE FUEL ECONOMY COMPARISON
www.fueleconomy.gov

Home

Organizations	
41Pounds www.41pounds.org	Will have your name removed from junk mail lists, for a fee
Debra's List www.debraslist.com	A clearinghouse of alternatives to common household toxics
Direct Mail Association www.dmachoice.org	Consumer information on direct mail from the trade association
Earth 911 www.earth911.org	Contains great information on recycling all types of material, with information on how to search for a recycler near you
GreenDimes www.greendimes.com	Will have your name removed from junk mail lists, for a fee
Water Quality Association www.wqa.org	Trade association for water filtration and treatment industry

Books	
Smith & Hawkin: The Hands-on Gardener: Composting Ball, Liz	Workman Publishing, New York, NY, 1997

Books continued	
Home Safe Home Dadd, Debra Lynn	Penguin Putnam, New York, NY, 1997
The Practical Organic Gardener Little, Brenda	Silverleaf Press, Sandy, UT, 2006
The World's Water 2004-2005 Gleick, Peter H.	Island Press, Washington DC, 2004
Water Wars Shiva, Vandana	South End Press, Cambridge, MA, 2002

Articles

"Non-Toxic Household Cleaners"
Central Vermont Solid Waste Management District
www.cvswmd.org/resident_services/cleaning-products.html

"Sorting out 'Green' Advertising Claims"
Federal Trade Commission
www.ftc.gov/bcp/edu/pubs/consumer/general/gen02

"The Hazardless Home Handbook"
Oregon Deptartment of Environmental Quality and Metro
www.metro-region.org/index.cfm/go/by.web/id=1400

Web Sites

CONSUMER REPORTS' ECO-LABELS CENTER

www.greenerchoices.org/eco-labels/eco-home.cfm

DIRECT MARKETING ASSOCIATION MAIL PREFERENCE SERVICE

www.dmachoice.org/MPS/proto1.php

NATIONAL DO NOT CALL REGISTRY

www.donotcall.gov

www.epa.gov/OGWDW/faq/faq.html

EPA: RADON

www.epa.gov/radon

METRO: GREEN CLEANERS

www.metroregion.org/index.cfm/go/by.web/id=1400

RECYCLED CONTENT PRODUCTS DIRECTORY

www.ciwmb.ca.gov/RCP/

AMERICAN CHEMISTRY COUNCIL: RECYCLED PLASTICS PRODUCT DIRECTORY

www.americanchemistry.com/s_plastics/sec_rppd.asp

PORTLAND WATER BUREAU: BATHROOM CONSERVATION TIPS

www.portlandonline.com/WATER/index.cfm?c=dafda

PORTLAND WATER BUREAU: WATER CONSERVATION TIPS

www.portlandonline.com/WATER/index.cfm?c=29594

General

Organizations	
ADVENT CONSPIRACY www.adventconspiracy.org	Promotes worshiping God through compassion, not consumption; currently over thirty churches in the U.S. are participants
EQUAL EXCHANGE www.equalexchange.com	Importer of Organic and Fair Trade commodities, including coffee, sugar, cocoa, chocolate
EVANGELICAL ENVIRON-MENTAL NETWORK www.creationcare.org	Publishes *Creation Care* magazine and many other resources for Christians and churches
KAPEH-UTZ www.kapeh-utz.com	Importer of Organic Fair Trade Coffee
NATIONAL ASSOCIATION OF EVANGELICALS www.nae.net	A broad organization representing sixty denominations and 45,000 churches
SUSTAINABLE HARVEST www.sustainableharvest.com	Importer of Organic Fair Trade Coffee

Books	
A Greener Faith Gottlieb, Roger S.	Oxford University Press, New York, NY, 2006

Books continued	
An Inconvenient Truth Gore, Al	Rodale, New York, NY, 2006
Another Turn of the Crank Berry, Wendell	Counterpoint, Washington DC, 1995
By Chance? MacMurray, John	Multnomah, Sisters, OR, 1998
Caring for Creation Oelschlaeger, Max	Yale University Press, New Haven, CT, 1994
Desert Solitaire Abbey, Edward	Touchstone, New York, NY, 1968
Earth Under Fire Braasch, Gary	University of California Press, Berkeley, CA, 2007
Go Green, Live Rich Bach, David with Rosner, Hillary	Broadway Books, New York, NY, 2008
Heaven Alcorn, Randy	Tyndale House, Wheaton, IL, 2004
How to Rescue the Earth *Without Worshipping Nature* Campolo, Tony	Thomas Nelson, Nashville, TN, 1992

Books continued

Hurtling Toward Oblivion Swenson, Richard A., MD	NavPress, Colorado Springs, CO, 1999
Issues Facing Christians *Today* Stott, John	4th Edition, Zondervan, Grand Rapids, MI, 2006
Nature, God & Pulpit Achtemeier, Elizabeth	William B. Eerdmans, Grand Rapids, MI, 1992
Pollution and the Death *of Man* Schaeffer, Francis A.	Tyndale House, Wheaton, IL, 1970
Redeeming Creation Van Dyke, Fred & Others	InterVarsity Press, Downers Grove, IL, 1996

Saving God's Green Earth
    Robinson, Tri with
    Chatraw, Jason
	Ampelon, Norcross, GA, 2006

Serve God, Save the *Planet* Sleeth, J. Matthew, MD	Zondervan, Grand Rapids, MI, 2007
The Best Preaching *on Earth* LeQuire, Stan L.	Judson Press, Valley Forge, PA, 1996

249

Books continued	
The Call of Creation MacMurray, John	Creation Calendars, Inc., Eagle Creek, OR, 2005
The Care of Creation R. J. Berry	InterVarsity Press, Downers Grove, IL, 2000
The Creation Wilson, E. O.	W.W. Norton and Company, New York, NY, 2006
The End of Nature McKibben, Bill	Anchor Books, New York, NY, 1990
The Green Book Rogers, Elizabeth and Kostigen, Thomas	Three Rivers Press, New York, NY, 2007
The Language of God Collins, Francis S.	Free Press, New York, NY, 2006
The Lorax Dr. Seuss	Random House, New York, NY, 1971
The Politically Incorrect Guide to Global Warming and Environmentalism Horner, Christopher C.	Regnery Publishing, Washington DC, 2007

250

Books continued

The World's Water 2004-2005 Gleick, Peter H.	Island Press, Washington DC, 2004
What Are People For? Berry, Wendell	North Point Press, New York, NY, 1990
While Creation Waits Larsen, Dale and Sandy	Harold Shaw, Wheaton, IL, 1992
Worldchanging: A User's Guide for the 21st Century Steffen, Alex	Abrams, New York, NY, 2006

Articles

"Restoring the Scandal of Christmas"
McKinley, Rick
Creation Care, Fall 2007, No. 34

Creation Care **Magazine**
4485 Tench Road, Suite 850, Suwanee, GA 30024
www.creationcare.org

Web Sites

Evangelical Climate Initiative
www.christiansandclimate.org/statement

251

Acknowledgments

Writing your first book is indeed a humbling experience. For all I know, it may be similar for your second, third, or thirtieth book. But a beginning author truly discovers how utterly dependent he is on others. Without knowledge, experience, or wisdom, he finds himself desperately calling out for help.

In my case, many people answered the calls. It started with my incredible wife, Vicki, and daughters Brooke and Maryn, who, from the very beginning, either really truly believed in me or were exceptionally talented actresses. Their enthusiasm to live as godly stewards of creation has been humbling. Quite simply, I am blessed above all other men.

A trio of dear friends were next to answer the call. Kevin, you are truly the iron that sharpens iron; your tough questions caused me to think deeper, reason more clearly, and care even more. As you have made me a better man for the past twenty-five years, you have likewise made this a much better book. Rob and Gary, your friendship and support played out with connections to people like Penny, John, and Randy who provided invaluable guidance along the way. These lovers of the Creator willingly sacrificed their time and talents for my benefit; I will never be able to thank them sufficiently. My literary advisors did the heavy slogging through early drafts and I am forever indebted to them: David, Kevin, Welby, John, Mike, Cindy, Ben, Jonathan, and Craig. Hopefully, this will be a more enjoyable read! Thank you all.

To my family on both sides—your words of encouragement and

prayers kept me going. You reminded me to be honest and real, and focused on the right things.

My most sincere thanks to Randy Alcorn. In spite of your incredible success as a minister, organizational leader, and author of both fiction and nonfiction, you took the time to encourage a fledgling writer with no "street cred" whatsoever. Your words of wisdom about writing, theology, and the publishing business were like tall glasses of water to a thirsty man. Thank you, Randy, for your generosity and commitment to kingdom work, whatever the personal cost.

None of this would have happened if I had not made a new friend along the way: Bill Jensen, you have been much more than my agent; you have been my most trusted advisor, my confidant and brother in Christ. Your insights were invaluable, and your creativity made this project sing. I hope to catch many more steelhead with you in the months and years ahead.

A rookie author must be the most challenging project for a publisher. The amazing folks at WaterBrook and Random House were nothing but encouraging maestros, helping me in countless ways. Mick, Pam, Jessica, Misty, and others behind the scenes, you are world-class handholders all. Thank you for your patience, your questions, your suggestions, and your willingness to take a risk with both the topic and the author.

To my friends and co-workers at GreenWorks and the city of Gresham: thank you all for your encouragement and interest, even when it seemed nonsensical. I didn't even notice you scratching your heads or raising your eyebrows. I realize that you had to make sacrifices so that this book could happen, and I'm grateful.

Along the way, I have been inspired by the many people who have been raising the banner for "creation care" for years, decades, and centuries: from St. Francis to Francis Schaeffer, Wendell Berry to John Stott, Matthew Sleeth to Francis Collins, many courageous people of faith have refused to stay in dogmatic political ruts—instead, they have insisted that Christians are to care for people and the planet.

Finally, and most importantly, I am eternally indebted to the Creator of it all. The Awesome One who breathed the Universe into life also took the time to inspire me personally. This is a great mystery—why the One who created all and controls all should care one whit about the most insignificant aspects of his creation—namely you and me. Yet, He does, and my life is so blessed because of His patient prodding:

Lord God, Creator of this unfathomable universe, incredible planet, and delightful creek upon which I live: Thank you for showing me your character, power, and beauty through all you have made. May my family, friends, and I answer Your call.

About the Author

A nationally recognized expert in green development strategies, Michael Abbaté, LEED™, ASLA, is a founder of Green-Works, an award-winning landscape architecture design firm. He frequently speaks to community leaders about practical ways to minimize the impact of development on natural resources and processes. Currently Urban Design and Planning Director for Gresham, Oregon, his works have been featured in national magazines, newspapers, and trade publications. He and his wife, Vicki, have two adult daughters and live near Portland.

This book was printed on recycled paper called Norbrite Book Cream. It is acid free and contains 20 percent postconsumer waste.